Reality According to the Scriptures

Initial Reflections

Reality According to the Scriptures

Initial Reflections

Inhabiting God's Story
An Interdisciplinary Exploration of Life in God's World
Volume 1

José Soto

WF
Wayfinders Publishing House
Natick, MA

Published by *Wayfinders Publishing House*
841 Worcester St. #153, Natick, MA 01760
www.wayfinders.press

Printed in the United States of America

Library of Congress Control Number: 2022906908

ISBN: 978-0-578-28991-5 (paperback)

ISBN: 978-0-578-28866-6 (e-book)

The cover image captures Isaiah 2:1–8 on The Great Isaiah Scroll (1QIsaa), ca. 125 BCE, digitized by Ardon Bar Hama. The Scroll is housed at the Shrine of the Book, The Israel Museum, Jerusalem. The image on the cover was provided by the Museum, and it's used with their permission. For more information, including an interactive image of the scroll, visit http://dss.collections.imj.org.il/isaiah.

Special thanks to gracelife.org for their Scripture indexing tool, which made the Scripture Index possible.

Lord Jesus
This is for you

My son, if you accept my words
and store up my commands within you,
turning your ear to wisdom
and applying your heart to understanding
—indeed, if you call out for insight
and cry aloud for understanding,
and if you look for it as for silver
and search for it as for hidden treasure,
then you will understand the fear of the LORD
and find the knowledge of God.

(Prov 2:1–5)

Trust in the LORD with all your heart
And do not lean on your own understanding.
In all your ways acknowledge Him,
And He will make your paths straight.

(Prov 3:5–6 NASB)

Contents

PART III
Getting Our Story Straight

INTRODUCTION

I hear the Scriptures telling a complex yet coherent Story of which we are a part. If this is so, then being at home in that Story must be a foundational and necessary aspect of what it means to be God's people. This little book is an invitation into that narrative-world.[1]

The present book is the first volume in a series of studies seeking to illuminate the nature and content of the gospel, to map the gospel onto the rest of reality, and to make the whole both comprehensible and inhabitable.

Part one of this volume begins the whole project by exploring the contours of a Christian approach to reality: one that takes into account the biblical claims about the nature of things, of course, but also all that we have learned about the world through science, history, and human experience in general.

Part two is a set of reflections on the nature and content of the gospel. Only a few themes were investigated in these studies (why exactly the gospel is good news, how it is that the death of Jesus could be considered a victory, and the Presence of God in the lives of his people); but these chapters also shed light on the internal logic of the biblical Story as a whole, and our place in it.

Much more will need to be said about the gospel in the rest of the series, but this much is clear already: that it is big—cosmic in fact, and that no place on earth or in heaven, and no aspect of our existence, escapes its reach. At this point, I would summarize it like this: *that absolutely all authority in heaven and on earth*

---

[1] When I capitalize the biblical Story, I have Reality in mind, which is what I hear the Scriptures claim to describe. When I refer to the biblical story in lower case, I mean the narrative of the Bible, without philosophical implications in mind.

has been given to the One who gave his life for us. That's the gospel in a nutshell. And it's very good news indeed.

Part three closes the volume with a single chapter reflecting on the need to get our Story straight. Besides some general considerations, I highlight a few areas on which I believe we've gone astray. In the rest of the project, we'll seek to sort it all out, as faithful stewards of the good news the world so desperately needs.

José Soto
Resurrection Day 2022

PART I
Inhabiting Reality

We human beings are unable to survive, and certainly cannot thrive, unless we can make meaning. If life is perceived as utterly random, fragmented, and chaotic—meaningless— we suffer confusion, distress, stagnation, and finally despair. The meaning we make orients our posture in the world, and determines our sense of self and purpose. We need to be able to make some sort of sense out of things; we seek pattern, order, coherence, and relation in the dynamic and disparate elements of our experience. —Sharon Daloz Parks[1]

---

[1] Sharon Daloz Parks, *Big Questions, Worthy Dreams: Mentoring Emerging Adults in Their Search for Meaning, Purpose, and Faith*, rev. ed. (San Francisco: Jossey-Bass, 2011), p. 10.

[*] *In the rest of the book, all notes and citations will be found in endnotes, at the end of each chapter.*

CHAPTER 1
A Christian Approach to Reality

All creation is a burning bush of the Lord God, revealing his just, merciful presence by the praise of countless creatures. —Calvin Seerveld[1]

How do I make sense of the world, and of myself? How do I find my way in the world? As I live these questions, and reflect on them, I discover myself in three conditions: a state of wonder at the marvel of the things I encounter and at the overabundant love of God to which I believe all these things testify; a state of heartbreak at the evil that vandalizes all things and that I discover (most often as misguided love) resident in myself; a state of hope when I discover that it (sometimes, in some ways) gets better and when I hear the promise in the apocalyptic poetry of the Bible that in the end all will be well. —Gideon Strauss[2]

"How do I find my way in the world?" This is one of the most beautiful and most promising questions I have ever heard. Beautiful because it evokes our deep longing to make sense out of things and be at home in the universe. Promising because it reframes our search for understanding in terms of our *being* in the world, and nothing less.

As I tried to answer that question here, I identified seven distinct elements to the way I make sense of things:

1. The lens of our experience
2. Inhabiting the biblical Story

3. Worldview analysis
4. The phenomenological lens
5. The social construction of reality
6. Minding the formative power of habit
7. And a biblical metaphysic

In this chapter, I'll unpack what I mean by each of these "lenses" and aspects of my approach to reality; I'll say a bit about how I came to this *multidimensional* way of looking at things; and I'll share the sources I found most helpful along the way.

I propose this framework as a biblical and Christian way to approach all of life and reality. The rest of the volume, and the rest of the series, should help test the framework's validity and its usefulness. By the end of the project we should have an even better version, but I'm already finding these resources quite helpful.

A note on sources
Theologians usually refer to four main sources or resources of Christian belief: *Scripture, tradition, reason,* and *experience.* So let me first explain where those four sources fit in my framework.[3]

1. My primary approach to *Scripture* will be explained below: I inhabit it, because I hear it telling a coherent Story of which I am a part.

2. Now, I couldn't understand the Scriptures rightly without the Christian *tradition,* without the guidance of those who came before me and passed on the biblical witness to us. I still have a lot to learn about the Christian tradition, but I'm working on it. I share a bit on that below. I want to get to know the church fathers and be more and more at home in church history, as Roman Catholics and other traditions have always enjoyed. Of course, I have to sort out truth from error, but that's with the aim

of embedding myself in the tradition—integrating the whole Story coherently so I can find myself in it. There's something deeply healing and nourishing about that prospect. In fact, I live for that.

3. The place of *experience* in my framework will be explained in the first and fourth sections below: given my approach to reality *from within,* my experience is where it all begins for me.

> The first philosophical act would appear to be to return to the world of actual experience which is prior to the objective world, since it is in it that we shall be able to grasp the theoretical basis no less than the limits of that objective world, restore to things their concrete physiognomy, to organisms their individual ways of dealing with the world, and to subjectivity its inherence in history. Our task will be, moreover, to rediscover phenomena, the layer of living experience through which other people and things are first given to us, the system "Self-others-things" as it comes into being; to reawaken perception and foil its trick of allowing us to forget it as a fact and as perception in the interest of the object which it presents to us and of the rational tradition to which it gives rise. —Maurice Merleau-Ponty, *Phenomenology of Perception*[4]

Although in this discussion I am engaging the experiential lens mostly in terms of personal and immediate experience, science, history, and human experience in general are equally important sources in this framework.

4. Finally, in all that follows you can assume that I'm trying to *reason!* In terms of *how* I reason, you can consider me a realist: a post-critical realist with a critical realist tool kit.

As Wendy Olsen explains, "the integration of the researcher-as-intentional-agent with the object of research as a 'real' thing is what critical realism has been working on..." and it's a key aspect of what I'm working on in this project.[5] Andrew Wright's description of a "critical religious education" further explains critical realism, and to a large extent captures my own approach to learning in general:

> Critical religious education is maximally committed to ontological realism, and maximally resistant to reductive accounts of the ultimate nature of reality. At the same time it seeks to be maximally committed to epistemic relativity, and maximally resistant to all forms of premature epistemic closure. This is in sharp contrast to both confessional and liberal approaches to the subject. Confessional religious education is maximally committed to ontological realism, but only minimally committed to epistemic relativity: the Transcendent reality confessed is treated as a given norm, and questions about its veracity are downplayed. Liberal religious education, on the other hand, is maximally committed to epistemic relativity, and only minimally committed to ontological realism: skepticism about Transcendent reality effectively excludes the pursuit of ultimate truth. Critical religious education's commitment to ontological realism frequently brings the charge of neo-confessionalism. However, this charge makes little sense when read in the light of critical religious education's equally trenchant commitment to epistemic relativity: particular theologies, universal theologies, the secular matrix of naturalism, humanism and liberalism, and indeed any other account of the ultimate order-of-things—including forms of ontological anti-realism—are all firmly on the agenda for debate. Thus the first 'critical' feature of critical religious education is its commitment to ontological realism about the ultimate order-of-things and our relation to it.[6]

However, I said above that I'm a *post*-critical realist, and that's because my stance toward reality is not fundamentally *critical*. I first discovered the possibility of what I call "traction on reality" thanks to critical realism (beginning with N. T. Wright's *The New Testament and the People of God),*[7] but that's not the only option. Later, I discovered the work of Esther Meek and, through her, Michael Polanyi's "post-critical" realism.[8] Perhaps given my approach to reality *from within,* I feel more at home in Polanyi's vision. Let me explain.

I'm post-critical because critical thinking and critical tools only give us access to one angle on reality: the focal. And it's only one approach to the focal too. Once we focus on what we're trying to understand, and start articulating what we see, we necessarily lose touch with much of its complexity and its richness: "unbridled lucidity can destroy our understanding of complex matters," as Polanyi puts it.[9]

You see, our bodies are immersed in reality. We're already in touch with the real by virtue of our being part of it. That's why, as Polanyi says, "we know more than we can tell."[10] Of course we want focal clarity about the nature of things. But we want to sacrifice as little as possible of our intuitive grasp of things during our investigation. A critical methodology remains an important part of that, but a critical *stance* does not—a sense of wonder would be more like it!

> *Believe me, unless you change your whole outlook and become like little children, you will never enter into God's new world.* (Matt 18:3; cf. 11:25–26; 21:15–16)[11]

The Lens of Our Experience
Like every child, while growing up I tried to make sense of things *through the lens of my experience*. My parents and others would give me clues to what was going on, but it was my experi-

ence I longed to make sense of, and I expected to grasp things precisely through my experience. Unfortunately, I grew up in a very confusing environment and my search for understanding was often frustrated. I guess I haven't been deterred though. To this day, I continue to seek and expect understanding experientially. Now, let me try to unpack what I mean by that.

It means that whatever other sources and perspectives I find to make sense of things, my experience needs to square with it. My experience should confirm the claims of other sources and angles on things. I should be at home in the Story I have received from my tradition because I *recognize* in my experience what I have heard from those other sources about the nature of things. I also expect to discern at least something of the nature of things through acts of contemplation. And I expect empirical evidence (sooner or later) to verify (or disprove) both what I discern through acts of contemplation, and what I have received through other sources and lenses.

All this assumes two things: that there is only *one reality,*[12] and that the physical world is real and good. If Plato was right and the physical world was just a shadow of the truly good and truly real, then I wouldn't be so committed to my experience in this physical world.[13] But because God declared his creation "very good" (Gen 1), and is utterly committed to his physical creation (to the point of becoming one of us!), I *am* at home in the land of the living and my experience in it matters.

My experience also matters because I was made to *relate,* not only to God but to the rest of his creation. Indeed, I was made to love (Deut 6:4–5; Lev 19:18; Mark 12:30–31)—to be *for the other,* which is the true meaning of "love."[14]

So, whatever else there is to the nature of things, of both the physical and the spiritual, it all belongs together—everything affecting everything else (cf. Col 1: 17). And all that is was set in motion by the One who's "making all things new" (Rev 21:5).

All things, then—past, present, and future—belong in this one picture. Reality is one, it seems to me, and my experience *within it* should give me access *to it,* however limited.[15]

By the way, I will probably adopt at least some elements of Bernard Lonergan's *experiential* approach, as expressed in his *Method in Theology*.[16] Regarding the *spiritual dimension* of reality, I'm finding the work of Michael Heiser most helpful.[17]

Inhabiting the Biblical Story

Later on, when I became a Christian, I started to make sense of my experience in light of God's Word. Eventually, it became clear that this meant locating myself *in* the biblical Story. I interpret my experience in light of the biblical Story because I believe that narrative describes and explains the world I inhabit.

You see, this Story claims that "In the beginning God created the heavens and the earth" (Gen 1:1). Clearly, there's nothing outside "the heavens and the earth," so the author of this text is himself a character in the Story he's telling. And so are we. Christian discipleship and evangelism, therefore, have everything to do with making this Story comprehensible *as reality,* and learning to live within it.[18]

This is part of what George Lindbeck means by his "intratextual" approach, as expressed in *The Nature of Doctrine*.[19] Lindbeck explicitly offers his approach as more promising than Lonergan's "experiential-expressivist" method, but I don't see why I should have to choose between the two.

I can see rejecting aspects of either or both of these approaches—whatever flaws I discover in their analyses.[20] But *I am* in God's Story. My experience is an experience *within* the narrative-world of the Bible. Therefore, I try to make sense of things through both lenses. That's why I consider this a multidimensional approach:

I need an *experiential* account (Lonergan) of the Story I *inhabit* (Lindbeck). Aren't these just two angles on the same reality: one from within looking out, and one from outside looking in? Not that I can stand outside the Story, but God can, and he reveals it to us so we can find ourselves in it.

Worldview Analysis

One way I find myself in God's Story is by answering worldview questions according to it, as explained by Walsh and Middleton in *The Transforming Vision*: Who am I? Where am I? What's wrong? and What's the solution?[21] These questions help me see the Story from within, through the lens of my experience, so I can find my way in God's world.

Worldview questions also provide a helpful point of contact between those who inhabit different stories. That point of contact is *faith*. All humans have to answer worldview questions, one way or another. But we can't find answers to such questions inside ourselves. These are questions about the ultimate order of things, and we haven't been outside the system to tell where it all came from and why we're here. We all need to *trust* some source or other for answers to such questions. This puts me on level ground with all humans on earth: we're all trusting creatures, creatures of faith.

When it comes to ultimate meaning, then, it's basically a matter of comparing sources. Who are *your* sources? And who are your sources' sources?

The Phenomenological Lens

I also engage my *experiential* lens within our Story when I allow myself to encounter reality *as it is*. That is, before making judgements, "bracketing" my presuppositions temporarily in my encounters with the real.[22]

> The phenomenological idea of going to the things themselves means to do full justice to the everyday experience, to the lived experience. ... 'Going to the things' [Husserl] means that, as researchers, we should position ourselves so the things can show themselves to us. —Karin Dahlberg, *Reflective Lifeworld Research*[23]

The phenomenological lens also helps me find my way in God's world because it keeps me alive to reality—to what's actually going on in the Story here and now. It helps me appreciate and come to know the nature of things *personally*, in my face-to-face encounters with them. Call it the *sense of wonder* for which the Giver of Life made us.

The Social Construction of Reality

Related to the *intratextual* approach is the fact that God wants us to create the world we want to inhabit, just as he's creating the cosmos he wants to inhabit (Gen 1:1, 26–28). This is an important aspect of God's Story because this creative freedom makes us co-authors with God: as children of God, made in his image and likeness to share in his life, we're actually co-writing his Story as we live it.[24]

I find it a key insight to know that God gave us the world culturally naked. That much of reality as we experience it is a social construction: a dense web of meaning that *we* have created through the ages, beginning with our use of language. To think that God gave us a role in *shaping the horizons of the possible,* as Andy Crouch would say—what a fascinating responsibility![25] Children of God indeed.

It's also liberating to know that things *could* be otherwise, even at the level of culture and meaning, because it didn't *have* to be this particular way in the first place. In culture making, and hence in human *being,* the possibilities are endless. And we know that things could be much more in line with God's intentions for the work of his hands. So, it's empowering to know that, as humans, we have the power and the authority to build towards that. Towards the future. Toward God's own vision for the work of his hands.[26]

The Formative Power of Habit

I'm also aware of the formative power of habit, as explained by James K. A. Smith in his Cultural Liturgies,[27] and in *You Are What You Love*.[28] This relates to both the *experiential* and *intratextual* lenses.

I can come to understand reality experientially, breaking things down empirically and coming to discern the nature of phenomena as I experience it face-to-face. But I can also choose what sort of person, what sort of interpreter, *I* will become by being mindful and intentional about my habits and experiences.

We are formed by our experiences. Our brains, in fact, are constantly being physically re-wired by our experiences. And our experiences, by and large, are directed by our rituals and ingrained habits. So, the question is: Am I *enacting* the Story I claim to inhabit?

However, our habits are driven by our desires. So, the ultimate question is: Are my *desires* in line with the Story I claim to inhabit? This should bring me full circle in wholehearted and faithful allegiance to the One who revealed the Story in the first place.[29]

A Biblical Metaphysic

A metaphysic is an understanding and explanation of the nature of ultimate reality—of the ultimate order-of-things.[30] As someone located in the biblical Story, I have a *biblical* metaphysic.

Reality *is* the narrative-world of the Bible. Ultimate reality is God himself, *the One behind all things* (Gen 1:1). He and his intentions for the work of his hands, *that* is my metaphysic.

However, when I hear God described as the "Ground of Being," for example, I am not hearing biblical metaphysics.[31] Not quite. It's not that I don't find that sort of image helpful; to some extent I do. They get at something of the nature of things. Paul too found such language helpful—*sometimes* (e.g., Acts 17:28). But God is no "ground." He's a person. So, I don't dwell much on such images and ways of thinking because I want to know and relate to God as he actually is. And when I consider all that *he* has said and done, the picture that emerges of him is nothing like "ground." That's too static. It's more like *a wise and loving Father!*

> [The Bible] depicts ultimate reality as not a thing or object or mere force or power but as someone who thinks, deliberates, acts, enters into relationships with others, responds to others, and has freedom to determine himself. And it depicts ultimate reality—that which is beyond appearance, upon which all else depends, the source of all that is—as more than nature, not part of nature, even the author of nature who is free to intervene in it. —Roger Olson, *The Essentials of Christian Thought*[32]

The Debate
There's a very important debate going on right now, about how much non-biblical Greek metaphysics has crept into Christian thought and culture through the centuries.[33] At this point I don't understand enough to have an informed stance in this conversation, but let me try to articulate where I am and what I'm learning, to give you a sense in what direction I might be going.[34]

Although I still have a lot to learn about the nature of the Christian tradition, it seems that the point of the tradition is to serve as parameters to guard and carry truth. It carries truth forward from generation to generation. And not just truth but also wisdom and ways of being and living according to it. Ways of enacting the Story it tells. If this is so, then the tradition is not an end in itself. It's a vehicle. Each generation must unpack what it carries and live it out on the ground. As some scholars say: "God has no grandchildren." He wants to father us himself.

So, what happens when we detect extra-biblical schemas in the construals of reality of the church fathers? Don't we need to make sure these new elements are in line with what God has been revealing from the beginning about himself, about the nature of things, and about his intentions for the work of his hands?

It seems to me that if we have to question the fathers, we must do it with reverence. For one thing, we're talking about siblings discussing what was helpful and not so helpful about our forebears' teaching and example. At least in general, we cherish what they have handed down to us. And it is precious. Even sacred. My dad and I, for example, don't even have much in common when it comes to matters of faith (not yet anyway!). But if for that reason I were to reject the wisdom he has gathered throughout his life, that would be an enormous shame. God forbid.

However, I need to be clear about what is actually true and real and good about his perspective and his example, *and only keep that.* Not just for myself, but for the sake of my children and my children's children. In a similar way, it seems to me, we need to sort out what we have received from our spiritual ancestors: honoring them, sorting with fear and trembling (knowing that the Spirit of God was at work in their lives too), but sorting things out nonetheless.

The Possibilities

I also think that we should not limit ourselves to the questions the fathers had to face. Each generation can expect new questions to emerge in their context and situation. Or did the fathers exhaust the faith? They tackled vital questions and settled many important matters for us. Of course they left us treasures. But there's a whole lot more to the apostolic tradition!

The creeds, for example, represent the culmination of a *particular* trajectory that the apostolic tradition took. But the creeds don't exhaust the tradition. Marianne Meye Thompson explains that the "creedal trajectory" begins in the New Testament and culminates with the creeds.[35] The creeds themselves point to the much larger "eschatological trajectory" of the apostolic tradition: to the *Life everlasting* of which they speak. All that we have received—indeed, church history itself—belongs *within* this eschatological trajectory: a trajectory that begins with God's promises in the Old Testament, and culminates in "a new heaven and a new earth" (Rev 21:1–4; cf. Isa 65:17–25).

That church history itself belongs within the biblical Story seems clear to me by the fact that there are promises and predictions in the Bible that still haven't been fulfilled. And this insight, this fact, is itself part of the tradition. Luke makes this clear, in Luke–Acts, by the way he adapted the tradition he received (from Mark) to clarify the crucial role the church plays *within* salvation history.[36]

> In various subtle ways, Luke mutes the apocalyptic trumpet that sounds from every page in Mark's Gospel. Luke's tempering of the tradition may best be seen by observing his redactional handling of the material that he inherited. ...
>
> By reducing the urgency of Jesus' expectation of the end and by pushing the day of judgment into an indefi-

15

nite future, Luke in effect creates an infinitely expanding historical "middle" in which the role of the church is paramount. As Joseph Fitzmyer puts it, Luke has sought "to shift Christian attention from an exclusive focus on imminence to a realization that the present Period of the Church also has place in God's salvation history." This making room for the church in history is one of Luke's most important contributions to New Testament theology and ethics. —Richard Hays, *The Moral Vision of the New Testament: Community, Cross, New Creation*[37]

If the tradition is not an end in itself but only a vehicle (as Luke knew when he tried to make sense of Mark), and if the fathers didn't exhaust the content and meaning of the faith, then it seems to me that in each generation the church needs to continue to discover and uncover more of its significance and its implications.

Of course, we're not going to do what Luke did to the tradition. The canon is closed. But as we discover and uncover more of its significance and its implications, we'll necessarily continue to shape it—to enrich it—as we live it out on the ground generation after generation.

As a living and dynamic aspect of the Christian faith, the church's tradition is always in the process of development, while providing stability in its canonical aspects. It has functioned as a kind of ongoing conversation that the church has had with itself for over two millennia, enabled by the Holy Spirit. The perennial flexibility and constancy of tradition (or traditioning) enable the church to address contemporary culture with the good news of the gospel. The article produced during Vatican II known as Dei Verbum states this progressive dynamic most usefully:

This tradition which comes from the Apostles develops in the Church with the help of the Holy Spirit. For there is a growth in the understanding of the realities and the words which have been made by believers, who treasure these things in their hearts (see Luke 2:19, 51), through a penetrating understanding of the spiritual realities which they experience... For as the centuries succeed one another, the Church constantly moves forward toward the fullness of divine truth until the words of God reach their complete fulfillment in her.

Because it is a living entity, the church's tradition articulated over the ages is also subject to reform and renewal—a point on which Roman Catholics and evangelicals generally agree. —D. H. Williams, *Evangelicals and Tradition: The Formative Influence of the Early Church*[38]

As I understand it, we're not *looking to* reform the tradition. That's not a posture the apostles would have encouraged, I don't think. Rather, we value what we have received as precious, and we cling to it *just as it is* (2 Thess 2:15). Call it our *default posture.* Nevertheless, authentic biblical discipleship will necessarily enrich and develop the tradition by virtue of our living it out. Call it our *default responsibility!* Only so can the tradition continue to carry *the power of God for the life of the world to the very end of the age* (Matt 28:20; Rom 1:16). That's how we continue to *echo* the gospel, isn't it? That's how we keep the tradition alive and real, because we too have the Holy Spirit.

Let us practice, then. What is it that we have received? What is this gospel? And why exactly is it good news, both for us and for those who will come after us?

That God is who he is, *that* is the ultimate miracle. That is why his message is good news for all of his creation. Add to that that he made us in his image, that he became one of us, that he gave his life for us, that he's making all things new. The significance and implications of this, it seems to me, are inexhaustible. Just as the possibilities in human being—in imaging God—in both his creative and his redemptive purposes, are inexhaustible.

The fathers did their part, no doubt. May we do ours too and make them proud. The point is to track with God and what he's up to, isn't it? How can our joy be complete if we lose sight of that?

---

[1] Calvin Seerveld, *Rainbows for the Fallen World: Aesthetic Life and Artistic Task* (Downsview, ON: Toronto Tuppence Press, 1980), p. 17.

[2] From Strauss' bio at the Institute for Christian Studies in Toronto, ON, accessed March 21, 2020, https://faculty.icscanada.edu/gstrauss. See also, Gideon Strauss, "Wonder, Heartbreak and Hope (7)," *Capital Commentary.* Center for Public Justice, 28 Jan. 2011– 23 Feb. 2011. https://cpjustice.org/public/capital_commentary/article/836.

[3] See also John G. Stackhouse Jr., *Need to Know: Vocation as the Heart of Christian Epistemology* (New York: Oxford University Press, 2014), where he speaks of five resources that include experience, tradition, Scripture, scholarship, and art. He considers *reason* a "mode of apprehension and consideration," along with *intuition* and *imagination.* I think that's a helpful improvement to John Wesley's quadrilateral, which had improved his Anglican theological tradition by adding *experience* to the original three components.

[4] Maurice Merleau-Ponty, *Phenomenology of Perception,* trans. Donald Landes (New York: Routledge, 2012), p. 66.

[5] Wendy Olsen, "Critical Realist Explorations in Methodology," *Methodological Innovations Online* 2, no. 2 (August 1, 2007): 1–5, https://doi.org/10.4256/mio.2007.0007.

[6] Andrew Wright, *Religious Education and Critical Realism: Knowledge, Reality and Religious Literacy* (New York: Routledge, 2015), p. 214.

[7] N. T. Wright, *The New Testament and the People God,* Christian Origins and The Question of God, vol. 1 (Minneapolis: Fortress Press, 1992).

[8] Esther Lightcap Meek, *Contact with Reality: Michael Polanyi's Realism and Why It Matters* (Eugene, OR: Cascade Books, 2017).

[9] Michael Polanyi, *The Tacit Dimension* (Gloucester, MA: Peter Smith, 1983), p. 18.

[10] Ibid., p. 4.

[11] Translated with the help of Barclay Moon Newman and Philip C. Stine, *A Handbook on the Gospel of Matthew*, UBS Helps for Translators (New York: United Bible Societies, 1992); J. B. Phillips, *The New Testament in Modern English* (New York: Collins, 1972); and *Today's German Bible* (Stuttgart: American Bible Society, 2001).

[12] See, for example, Graham Priest, *One Being: An Investigation into the Unity of Reality and of Its Parts, Including the Singular Object Which Is Nothingness* (New York: Oxford University Press, 2016), where he explains "what it means for all things to be one" (p. xvii). See also Andrew Wright, *Religious Education and Critical Realism,* p. 202: "Our best (currently) available retroductive account suggests that we participate in a single reality that is constituted by the totality of all that exists, once existed and potentially might exist. We experience and explain this reality as stratified, emergent, transfactual and causally efficacious. Though everything is interconnected in a thick web of causality, the fact that higher strata are irreducible to the lower strata from which they emerge requires us to recognise the existence of distinct-yet-related domains of being." All I mean though is that there's only one reality, however complex. A colleague once objected that this couldn't be because there may be many universes, not just one. I answered that if there are many universes, then *that* is reality. It remains one. As Andrew Wright explains: "To the best of our knowledge, everything in reality is ontologically related. If alternative realities other than our own exist then they must be ontologically related to our reality, even if that relationship is a negative relationship of absolute disconnectedness" (ibid., p. 214).

[13] Plato, *The Republic,* trans. Desmond Lee (London: Penguin Classics, 2007), 514a–520a.

[14] As James Olthuis put it: "Loving is not merely one thing among others that we are called to do—an extraordinary achievement, a heroic gesture

that completes ordinary acts and raises them to a higher level. Love is not an additive, a spiritual supplement reserved for saints, for those few consecrated to some higher purpose. Loving is of the essence of being human, the connective tissue of reality, the oxygen of life... God's love is the oxygen that sustains the universe, the glue cohering the universe, the fire impassioning the universe. Love calls us—claims us—to responsibility, engagement, and mutuality. In the brokenness of sin and evil, love calls us to repentance, reconciliation, and transformation. Without love, the ether of existence vaporizes, the fabric of life unravels." Olthuis, *The Beautiful Risk* (Grand Rapids: Zondervan, 2001), p. 69. See also Timothy R. Jennings, *The God-Shaped Brain: How Changing Your View of God Transforms Your Life* (Downers Grove: IVP, 2017), pp. 24–26. Here's an excerpt of Jennings' beautiful vision: https://www.wayfinders.quest/jennings.html.

[15] Sociologist Christian Smith explains the need "to replace the too-dominant image of humans as primarily *perceivers of* reality with the image of humans as *natural participants in* reality." The prevalent "background view of the human condition ... supposes humans as cut off from the real ... as somehow exiled from the true reality within which they live, primarily because of the alleged epistemic limitations of language." He explains that "this belief in our inescapably alienated condition was set up for us in part by Immanuel Kant's key distinction between 'noumenal' reality and 'phenomenal' reality—a disastrous move driven by a desire to preserve morality in a world of Newtonian determinism—that is, between things 'as they really are in themselves' and things as they merely appear to us. Noumenal reality no doubt exists out there, this account supposes, but we humans have no good access to it because all of our knowledge is limited by our restricted capacities of empirical perceptions. The only world we can ever reside in is the world of appearances. We are separated from the world as it really is by an unbridgeable epistemic chasm." But "quite to the contrary, we humans are fully *participants in* reality, a reality that is not identical to us but still fully ours. We emerge from, consist of, belong to, and are intricately connected with the totality of reality, material and otherwise. ... Because we belong to and participate in reality, because we 'indwell' reality, as Michael Polanyi said, rather than merely observing it, over the years we develop a profound 'tacit knowledge' of what reality is and how reality works. 'We know more than we can tell,' Polanyi observes. 'It is not by looking at things, but by dwelling in them, that we understand their ... meaning.' Thus, the real we seek to know is therefore not fundamentally concealed or removed from us. We are more than intimately part of it. It composes us. We participate in its natural operations. We are thus terrifically well positioned to know and understand it." Christian Smith, *What Is a Person?: Rethinking Humanity,*

Social Life, and the Moral Good from the Person Up (Chicago: University of Chicago Press, 2011), pp. 170–71, quoting Michael Polanyi, *The Tacit Dimension,* pp. 4, 18.

[16] Bernard Lonergan, *Method in Theology: Lonergan Studies,* 2nd ed. (Toronto, ON: University of Toronto Press, 2017). Here's an excerpt where he summarizes his approach: https://www.wayfinders.quest/lonergan.html.

[17] Michael S. Heiser, *Supernatural: What the Bible Teaches About the Unseen World—and Why It Matters* (Bellingham: Lexham Press, 2015); and Heiser, *The Unseen Realm: Recovering the Supernatural Worldview of the Bible* (Bellingham: Lexham Press, 2015). See also my initial reflections on the need to take into account the spiritual dimension of reality, as the Bible clearly does: https://www.wayfinders.quest/spiritual-dimension.html.

[18] I'm beginning to explore this theme on "Inhabiting God's Story: Initial Reflections:" https://www.wayfinders.quest/gods-story-reflections.html. For an excellent scholarly account of the nature of Scripture that's in line with my approach, see Iain Provan, *The Reformation and the Right Reading of Scripture* (Waco, TX: Baylor University Press, 2017).

[19] George A. Lindbeck and Bruce D. Marshall, *The Nature of Doctrine, 25th Anniversary Edition: Religion and Theology in a Postliberal Age* (Louisville, KY: Westminster John Knox Press, 2009).

[20] For example, it's possible that what I will end up embracing from Lindbeck (and the Yale School in general) is mostly the call to let the Bible "absorb the universe" (*The Nature of Doctrine,* p. 117): finding ourselves, and the rest of the cosmos, in the narrative-world of the Bible. I can already see that some of the ways in which theologians are using the philosophical and sociological insights that Lindbeck deploys are at odds with my reading of Scripture and my use of these insights. Proponents of "fictionalism," as some call it, believe that "religious concepts have meaning only in relation to the other concepts of the religion to which they belong and no meaning outside of that socio-linguistic system." Douglas V. Porpora, "A Propaedeutic to a Propaedeutic on Inter-Religious Dialogue," in *Transcendence: Critical Realism and God* (New York: Routledge, 2004), p. 111. I'm not sure about other religions (we'll probably investigate that later on in this series), but this statement does not square with the claims of the biblical texts themselves. I do appreciate the philosophical and sociological insights behind their approach, but I'm taking them in a different direction. The Bible claims to describe reality and its ultimate meaning, and not just for those who inhabit its narrative-world, since it judges all other accounts of reality according to how they square with

what the Creator himself has revealed about the nature of things. That is, the biblical Story claims to be relevant to everyone and to all of creation, since it describes the origins and destiny of all things. Its concepts are thus relevant and explicable to unbelievers, and can also be meaningful to them, as long as the believers who explain them actually know what they're talking about. See also George A. Lindbeck, Dennis L. Okholm, and Timothy R. Phillips, eds., *The Nature of Confession: Evangelicals & Postliberals in Conversation* (Downers Grove: Intervarsity Press, 1996); and James K. A. Smith, *Who's Afraid of Relativism?: Community, Contingency, And Creaturehood* (Grand Rapids: Baker Academic, 2014), ch. 5, "The (Inferential) Nature of Doctrine: Postliberalism as Christian Pragmatism."

[21] Brian J. Walsh and J. Richard Middleton, *The Transforming Vision: Shaping a Christian World View* (Downers Grove: IVP Academic, 1984). On worldview studies, see also David Rousseau and Julie Billingham, "A Systematic Framework for Exploring Worldviews and Its Generalization as a Multi-Purpose Inquiry Framework," *Systems* 6, no. 3 (September 2018): p. 27, https://doi.org/10.3390/systems6030027; and Ted Turnau, *Popologetics: Popular Culture in Christian Perspective* (Phillipsburg, NJ: P&R, 2012), ch. 1, sec. titled "The Trunk: The World-Story." Kindle ed.

[22] The most helpful guide I've found in the study and practice of phenomenology is Max van Manen, especially his *Phenomenology of Practice: Meaning-Giving Methods in Phenomenological Research and Writing* (New York: Routledge, 2014); and Max van Manen, ed., *Writing in the Dark: Phenomenological Studies in Interpretive Inquiry* (New York: Routledge, 2003).

[23] Karin Dahlberg, Helena Dahlberg, and Maria Nystrom, *Reflective Lifeworld Research*, 2nd ed. (Lund: Studentlitteratur AB, 2008).

[24] Much of this is helpfully explained by Andy Crouch, *Culture Making: Recovering Our Creative Calling* (Downers Grove: IVP, 2013). Crouch is indebted to Peter Berger and Thomas Luckmann, who broke these things down for us in *The Social Construction of Reality: A Treatise in the Sociology of Knowledge* (New York: Anchor, 1967). Lindbeck, above, is also indebted to them to some extent. And these insights by the sociology of knowledge are corroborated by Scripture too. See, for example, J. Gordon McConville, *Being Human in God's World: An Old Testament Theology of Humanity* (Grand Rapids: Baker Academic, 2016). Here's an excerpt from *Being Human*, ch. 9 (on work and creativity): https://www.wayfinders.quest/mcconville.html. See also my own reflections on "What Matters Most:" https://www.wayfinders. quest/what-matters-most.html; and in another connection, see my "Co-

Writing God's Story:" https://www.wayfinders.quest/co-writing-gods-story.
html; and also ch. 5, below: "The Body of Christ in a World of Competing
Narratives" (under "Introduction").

[25] Crouch, *Culture Making,* ch. 1.

[26] I should clarify that what I have in mind in this section is what's often called
"*weak* social constructionism," as opposed to the strong version. The weak
version, the "realist" version, as Christian Smith prefers to call it, "sounds
something like this: All human knowledge is conceptually mediated and
can be and usually is influenced by particular and contingent sociocultural
factors such as material interests, group structures, linguistic categories,
technological development, and the like—such that what people believe to
be real is significantly shaped not only by objective reality but also by their
sociocultural contexts. Furthermore, there is a dimension of reality that humans
socially construct, what I will refer to below as institutional facts, that is,
those aspects of the real that humans think, speak, and interact into existence.
This weak or realist version is an essential sociological insight crucial for
understanding human persons and social reality." As for the strong version,
it claims something like this: "Reality itself for humans is a human, social
construction, constituted by human mental categories, discursive practices,
definitions of situations, and symbolic exchanges that are sustained as 'real'
through ongoing social interactions that are in turn shaped by particular
interests, perspectives, and, usually, imbalances of power—our knowledge
about reality is therefore entirely culturally relative, since no human has
access to reality 'as it really is' (if such a thing exists or can be talked about
intelligibly) because we can never escape our human epistemological and
linguistic limits to verify whether our beliefs about reality correspond with
externally objective reality. This strong version of social constructionism is
fraught with problems. We should reject constructionism's strong version. I
think that many social constructionist sociologists would, if pressed, say that
they really believe in the weak version of constructionism. But for various
reasons many nevertheless seem recurrently to slip into statements that
appear to affirm the strong version instead. In short, many constructionist
analyses are often confusing in what they claim. Perhaps this is because they
are confused in what they think." Christian Smith, *What Is a Person?,* p. 122.
See also Ian Hacking, *The Social Construction of What?* (Cambridge, MA:
Harvard University Press, 1999).

[27] James K. A. Smith, *Desiring the Kingdom: Worship, Worldview, and
Cultural Formation* (Grand Rapids: Baker Academic, 2009); Smith, *Imagining
the Kingdom: How Worship Works* (Grand Rapids: Baker Academic, 2013);

and Smith, *Awaiting the King: Reforming Public Theology* (Grand Rapids: Baker Academic, 2017).

[28] James K. A. Smith, *You Are What You Love: The Spiritual Power of Habit* (Grand Rapids: Brazos, 2016).

[29] So, for example, Gideon Strauss adds the question of desire to his worldview analysis questions: "Who am I? Where do I belong? What is the world and what do I believe about it? *What do I love?* What opportunities and constraints do I face in my particular context? What am I to do with my life?" Strauss, "World-Viewing: An Introduction to Worldview Studies," ICS Courses, accessed February 17, 2022, http://courses.icscanada.edu/2018/08/world-viewing-introduction-to-worldview.html (emphasis added).

[30] See, for example, Roger E. Olson, *The Essentials of Christian Thought: Seeing Reality through the Biblical Story* (Grand Rapids: Zondervan, 2017).

[31] Wesley J. Wildman, "Ground-of-Being Theologies," in *The Oxford Handbook of Religion and Science,* ed. Philip Clayton (New York: Oxford University Press, 2006), pp. 612–32.

[32] Olson, *The Essentials of Christian Thought,* p. 54.

[33] Edwin Judge, "How the Debate Between Rome & Jerusalem Shaped the Modern World," accessed February 17, 2022, https://www.gospelconversations.com/series/edwin-judge; and this wonderful follow-up by Iain Provan, "Seriously Dangerous Religion" (lecture series), accessed February 17, 2022, https://www.gospelconversations.com/series/seriously-dangerous-religion; Hans Boersma and Rikk E. Watts, *Athens and Jerusalem: Philosophy and History Informing Christian Theology* (Regent College, Vancouver [BC, Canada], 2009), https://www.regentaudio.com/products/athens-and-jerusalem-philosophy-and-history-informing-christian-theology-a-dialogue; Rikk E. Watts, *Jerusalem Versus Athens Revisited: Why the 21st Century Is the Most Christian* (Regent College, Vancouver [BC, Canada], 2015), https://www.regentaudio.com/products/jerusalem-versus-athens-revisited-why-the-21st-century-is-the-most-christian-and-the-most-confused. See also Tom Holland, *Dominion: How the Christian Revolution Remade the World* (New York: Basic Books, 2019).

[34] Besides the sources I'll reference below, I found these resources helpful: Christopher Hall, *The Role of Tradition in Evangelical Theology* (Regent College, Vancouver [BC, Canada], 2005), https://www.regentaudio.com/products/the-role-of-tradition-in-evangelical-theology; and Mark Husbands, ed., *Ancient Faith for the Church's Future* (Downers Grove: IVP Academic, 2008). The work of Abraham Heschel can be helpful here too. See, for example,

Heschel, *Man Is Not Alone: A Philosophy of Religion* (New York: Farrar, Straus and Giroux, 1979). I love his beginning with wonder, by the way, though I myself might start with wisdom ("What is our life?") and then link to wonder. However, I'm not onboard with his treatment of *revelation* in this book. I'm actually surprised Heschel was able to see so much about *who God is* in his later works with such a low view of revelation. There's probably development (for the better, in my view) in his understanding of revelation from the publication of *Man Is Not Alone* (1951) to that of *The Prophets* (1962), for example. I don't know though, the man to ask would be Shai Held, *Abraham Joshua Heschel: The Call of Transcendence* (Bloomington, IN: Indiana University Press, 2015). Here's Heschel at his best: "The God of the philosophers is like the Greek *anankê,* unknown and indifferent to man; He thinks, but does not speak; He is conscious of Himself, but oblivious of the world; while the God of Israel is a God Who loves, a God Who is known to, and concerned with, man. He not only rules the world in the majesty of His might and wisdom, but reacts intimately to the events of history. He does not judge men's deeds impassively and with aloofness; His judgment is imbued with the attitude of One to Whom those actions are of the most intimate and profound concern. God does not stand outside the range of human suffering and sorrow. He is personally involved in, even stirred by, the conduct and fate of man. ... Sympathy opens man to the living God. Unless we share His concern, we know nothing about the living God." Heschel, *The Prophets* (New York: Harper & Row, 1962), p. 289.

[35] Marianne Meye Thompson, *The Promise of the Father: Jesus and God in the New Testament* (Louisville, KY: Westminster John Knox Press, 2000), p. 155ff.

[36] Most New Testament scholars believe Mark's was the first Gospel to be written, and also that Luke used Mark as a source. See for example, Darrell L. Bock, *A Theology of Luke and Acts: God's Promised Program, Realized for All Nations* (Grand Rapids: Zondervan, 2012). See also Robert H. Stein, *The Synoptic Problem: An Introduction* (Grand Rapids: Baker, 1987).

[37] Richard Hays, *The Moral Vision of the New Testament: Community, Cross, New Creation: A Contemporary Introduction to New Testament Ethic* (San Francisco: HarperOne, 1996), p. 131, quoting Joseph A. Fitzmyer, *The Gospel According to Luke I–IX: Introduction, Translation, and Notes* (Garden City, NY: Doubleday, 1981), p. 235.

[38] D. H. Williams, *Evangelicals and Tradition: The Formative Influence of the Early Church* (Grand Rapids: Baker Academic, 2005), p. 182, quoting Dei Verbum, II.8, in *The Documents of Vatican II*, ed. W. Abbott (New York: Association Press, 1966), p. 116.

PART II

Reality According to the Scriptures

Always be prepared to give an answer to everyone who asks you to give the reason for the hope that you have.

(1 Pet 3:15)

Concerning this salvation, the prophets, who spoke of the grace that was to come to you, searched intently and with the greatest care, trying to find out the time and circumstances to which the Spirit of Christ in them was pointing when he predicted the sufferings of the Messiah and the glories that would follow. It was revealed to them that they were not serving themselves but you, when they spoke of the things that have now been told you by those who have preached the gospel to you by the Holy Spirit sent from heaven. Even angels long to look into these things.

(1 Pet 1:10–12)

So do I. Let's get to it.

CHAPTER 2
The Gospel of Life

This has become one of the most significant themes in my understanding of the content of the gospel: *life* itself. I still agree with the psalmist that *God's love is better than life* (Ps 63:3). And in my universe, there's nothing better—no better news— than *who God is*. He's not only good, in a sense he's Goodness itself (Exod 33:18–23), and the gospel is good news first and foremost because it is *his* message. Nevertheless, at the heart of his message is an offer, and that offer is *life* (e.g., John 6:68; 10:10; 20:31; Rom 6:23; 1 John 2:25).[1]

This is the case both explicitly, as we find it in John 10:10 for example, and also implicitly, because God's message is latent in creation itself and in more than one way (cf. Rom 1:18–20).[2]

The Meaning of Life

There's an implicit message from God in the very fact of his creating us. Why did he make us? He made us because he wanted a family—intimate allies made in his image to care for this wonderful planet (e.g., Gen 1:26–28; cf. 5:1–3).[3] And what is the point of life in this planet? To what end do we care for it? The point of our life is actually *life itself,* both because "life is an end in itself," as Terry Eagleton rightly said,[4] and because God made us precisely *for* life (e.g., Gen 1; Deut 30:19–20; Ps 104; John 1:1–4; 10:10; Acts 14:15–17; 17:24–28). Our *call* to "care for this wonderful planet,"[5] in the context of *life-giving relationships* with God and one another,[6] that's all part of the *gift* of this life that we're made for.

> *In the beginning was the Word, and the Word was with*
> *God, and the Word was God. He was in the beginning*

with God. All things came into being through him, and without him not one thing came into being. What has come into being in him was life, and the life was the light of all people. (John 1:1–4 NRSV; cf. CEB)

What's more, this life God made us for is nothing less than his own life.[7] We are children of God by design (Gen 1:26–28; 5:1–3), made in his image and likeness, precisely to share in his life.[8] To think that we even share his breath (Gen 2:7), and even his breath is "the breath of life!"

At Home in God's World

Now, if I were to tell the gospel Story, as someday I hope to do, the metaphor of *home/homemaking* would probably be the overarching theme, since home is the *context* of life and life is the *content* of home. The cosmos is God's temple-palace, his home and ours too.[9] And it is first and foremost to be at home with him in this place that he made us. Talk about the content of the gospel, to me, is talk about the meaning of life.[10]

The Good News of the Gospel

In the rest of this chapter, I'm going to explain from a couple of different angles what I mean by "the gospel of life," beginning now with the initial intuition that eventually led to the reflections above: that the gospel is good news because at bottom it is about life.

Now, the first thing you might notice is that I was actually asking the question! And yes, for me it wasn't self-evident why the Christian gospel is good news. In most of the proclamations I had heard, the actual good news was only evident from within the framework in which it was presented. It did sound like good news once I understood where they were coming from. But their message was good news to me not so much because their *message* had struck me as great news, but because those communities themselves were good news to me.

Too often, though, they seemed to be answering questions I wasn't asking. It just wasn't clear why this message should strike me as good news; which, if it was indeed for me, it should.

But when I read the book of Acts, this didn't seem to be the case at the beginning. The world was turned "upside down" with this message (Acts 17:6 NRSV)! It had to be relevant to unbelievers from other nations. The message had to make sense to them. The reason why it is good news had to be evident to people, wherever they came from. So I kept digging, even as a Christian, out of existential necessity. And one of the most compelling reasons that's emerging for me is also the most basic: *life itself.*

That is, I am finding in the *gift* of life, in the *goodness* of life, a fundamental and essential reason why the gospel is good news for all of God's creation. More fundamental to the gospel than the Story that explains it. And more fundamental to the gospel than any particular expression of it. Why? Because in the Christian gospel life *is* the offer. *Life is the point,* actually, in both creation and redemption (e.g., John 1:1–4; 10:10; Rom 6:23).

My sense is that the writers of Scripture presupposed this, but we no longer do. Notice the content of Paul's message when he speaks to Gentile unbelievers.

> *The God who made the world and everything in it is the Lord of heaven and earth and does not live in temples built by human hands. And he is not served by human hands, as if he needed anything. Rather, he himself gives everyone life and breath and everything else. From one man he made all the nations, that they should inhabit the whole earth....* (Acts 17:22–28)

Here is a man who knows what he's talking about, and who's in touch with the needs of his audience (where they're coming from), and he goes straight to the point of it all: the very reason we exist, he says, is *that we should inhabit the earth.* We are made for life, plain and simple. The gospel is the message and the Story that announces and explains this wonderful reality— and Whose idea it was to bring it all about. Only then does it make sense as the message and the Story that explains why we need "salvation," and what's the nature and the scope of God's redemptive agenda. *God so loved the world that he gave his only Son* (John 3:16), yes, but before that, *God so loved the world that he made it* (Gen 1)!

> What is salvation but the outworking of God's love for his creation as he restores it from the bondage and effects of sin? Creation, then, although certainly not the central message of Scripture, is the underlying foundation. Indeed, without an understanding of the biblical view of creation our understanding of both sin and redemption will inevitably be distorted. In world-view terms, we cannot answer the questions "What's wrong?" and "What's the remedy?" unless we first address the issues of who we are and where we are.
> —Brian Walsh and Richard Middleton[11]

> God's work in the world must be viewed in and through a universal frame of reference. That the Bible begins with Genesis, not Exodus, with creation, not redemption, is of immeasurable importance for understanding all that follows. —Terence Fretheim[12]

Life Itself

Let's go a bit deeper though. Not only is *creation* the beginning of our Story, in a temporal sense, so that we have to start there to get the picture and know what's going on. We get even closer to what I have in mind when we realize that God's creation (the cosmos) is itself telling the Story.[13] Creation is in fact part of the message. God's message. And we, our lives and our words, are part of it. Part of that larger, quieter reality that from the beginning speaks for itself about who God is. Psalm 19 and Romans 1:18–20 are part of that witness.

> Our relationship to God is given in and with life itself. ... Man cannot live, without living from God. ... Whatever form it may take, man's relationship to God begins by being that of a creature who has been born, who lives, who never ceases to be created from first to last. As such he receives all that he has from the Creator, independently of what his attitude to the Creator may be, just as a son may receive from his natural father, even when he curses him. ... For this relationship is given with life itself, and even when men have ceased to use the term "God" they do not cease to be related to Him, because *He is,* even though they deny him. —Gustaf Wingren[14]

> *We are bringing you good news, telling you to turn from these worthless things to the living God, who made the heavens and the earth and the sea and everything in them. In the past, he let all nations go their own way. Yet he has not left himself without testimony: He has shown kindness by giving you rain from heaven and crops in their seasons; he provides you with plenty of food and fills your hearts with joy.* (Acts 14:15–17; cf. Ps 104)

All humans, believers or not, are already longing for God. We're all desperate for him, whether we know it or not. In the very love of life, we already know what he's all about, even if we haven't *recognized* him yet as the source of all we truly want.[15]

That's my sense. And it may well be what Paul is trying to tap here: *"Just open your eyes!"*

> In Genesis 1, a cue may be taken from God's repeated judgment on his works that they are "good." ... the Hebrew *ṭôb* can connote "beautiful" as well as "good" in a moral sense, and in this beginning of all things the divine assessment is essentially aesthetic. The world in its ordered profusion is beautiful. Since it is beautiful in the eyes of its maker, it reflects the thoughts of its maker, and so the maker himself. —Gordon McConville[16]

If I'm going to be an evangelist (as Grandma used to say I would), this is the context and the framework within which I'd like to witness. In the common ground of *God's creation.* Of common grace. A message that is good news about reality. About human *being.* About life. A gospel that is as simple as it is beautiful. And as real as it is unlikely. Like life itself. A true miracle.

Inhabiting God's Story

As I said in the Introduction, I hear the Scriptures telling a coherent Story of which we are a part. I've been thinking and praying a lot about this and what it might mean for us in practice. A key insight, one I will explore in what remains of this chapter, is that inhabiting the biblical Story doesn't happen at the level of the big picture, of the larger Story. The big picture itself sends us down to the *interpersonal* level, because that's where life happens.

Life happens here at the intersection of the big picture and the existential level of reality: what David Ford calls the "middle distance,"[17] which is Levinas' "face-to-face"[18] and David Kelsey's "quotidian,"[19] everyday life. Peter Berger and Thomas

Luckmann call it "paramount reality."[20] I call it "life on the ground."[21]

We want to know the larger Story well so that we're clear about who we are and what's going on. *So we can spot falsehood when we see it.* We want to remember history and trust God's promises for what's to come. We want to play our part well in that larger Story.

But the biblical Story itself locates us on the ground, loving our neighbor and caring for creation. Even loving God doesn't happen up there somewhere. It is fitting to lift our eyes and our hands to him in prayer and praise. He is above. But he's also here: *he who is behind all things is also here, on the ground, with us* (e.g., Isa 57:15). It is here that he's proved himself faithful. And it's here that we love and trust and obey him. Just as Jesus did.

This would seem obvious, but somehow I had missed it. Perhaps because of all the Platonism going on around me or something, I imagined living God's Story as somehow rising above "ordinary" life. But this can't be. *Our daily experience of life on this beautiful planet is what God intended for us when he created all things.* It is life on earth he's redeeming. This is home![22]

Inhabiting the Kingdom

And what about the kingdom of God? How does "the gospel of the kingdom" square with "the gospel of life"?

Well, it is clear in the New Testament that the kingdom had come through the Lord Jesus (e.g., Mark 1:14–15; Matt 24:14). So, what would *he* say the kingdom of God is all about? How did he live it out? What did his life and ministry look like?

It looked like blind people seeing, lame people walking, the guilty and shamed forgiven and restored so they could enjoy the gift of life with the rest of the community. He came to give us life, that's what he said and what he did (John 10:10; cf. Rom 6:23), and that's precisely what the kingdom of God is all about.

This is confirmed by John's understanding of the kingdom. While the Synoptic Gospels (Mark, Matthew, and Luke) record Jesus proclaiming the "kingdom of God," John the Evangelist shows Jesus talking about "life" and "eternal life." There seems to be a consensus among New Testament scholars that "eternal life" in John's Gospel functions as "kingdom of God" does in the other Gospels.[23] The kingdom is basically about God's will, about his intentions for his creation and his commitment to bring it about. And how did John proclaim this message? To capture God's intentions for the world, which in a very real sense *is* the good news of the gospel, John had to speak of nothing less than "life" itself.[24]

To Israel, "the kingdom of God" meant *shalom,* peace, justice, God's Presence again among his people, his promises finally realized, fullness of life at last. That's what God wants for us, and that is the offer of the gospel: fullness of life, here, in our lives—and a whole lot more to come after the resurrection (e.g., Rom 8:18–25; 1 Cor 15:12–14, 53–58).

Reinhabiting Life

To conclude then, inhabiting God's Story, and inhabiting his kingdom, is not something with do at the level of the big picture. We want to inhabit the larger Story of which we're a part, but this must happen on the ground, at the interpersonal level, where the drama of life goes on.

It's through *the lens of our experience of life* that we must zoom out to envision the big picture and then find ourselves there. Once there, we're still in our lives, where we belong; but now we're in a different Story, so our experience is transformed.

Now the truth of all the stories and the voices we had heard is tested by God's Story. We start to wake up to God's future for his world. And our present is transformed.

We re-imagine our lives, we reinhabit life, because we've found our way home.

---

[1] This chapter brings together various discussions I'm sharing at https://www.wayfinders.quest/the-gospel.html.

[2] See, for example, Terence E. Fretheim, *God and World in the Old Testament: A Relational Theology of Creation* (Nashville: Abingdon Press, 2005), ch. 8: "Nature's Praise of God."

[3] J. Richard Middleton, *A New Heaven and a New Earth: Reclaiming Biblical Eschatology* (Grand Rapids: Baker Academic, 2014), ch. 2: "Why Are We Here?: Being Human as Sacred Calling;" Rikk E. Watts, "The New Exodus/New Creational Restoration of the Image of God," in *What Does It Mean to Be Saved? Broadening Evangelical Horizons of Salvation*, ed. John G. Stackhouse Jr. (Grand Rapids: Baker Academic, 2002), pp. 15–41.

[4] Terry Eagleton, *The Meaning of Life: A Very Short Introduction* (New York: Oxford University Press, 2008), p. 94ff. There are some points on which I have to disagree with his proposal, but for the most part I'm onboard with it. For example, I don't think that because life is an end in itself "what we need is a form of life which is completely pointless, just as the jazz performance is pointless" (p. 100). But I see where he's coming from: "Rather than serve some utilitarian purpose or earnest metaphysical end, [life] is a delight in itself. It needs no justification beyond its own existence. In this sense, the meaning of life is interestingly close to meaninglessness [cf. Ecclesiastes]. Religious believers who find this version of the meaning of life a little too laid-back for comfort should remind themselves that God, too, is his own end, ground, origin, reason, and self-delight, and that only by living this way can human beings be said to share in his life. Believers sometimes speak as though a key difference between themselves and non-believers is that for them, the meaning and purpose of life lie outside it. But this is not quite

true even for believers. For classical theology, God transcends the world, but figures as a depth within it." Indeed, it is his home! "[In the gospel of Matthew] salvation turns out to be an embarrassingly prosaic affair – a matter of feeding the hungry, giving drink to the thirsty, welcoming the stranger, and visiting the imprisoned. It has no 'religious' glamour or aura whatsoever. Anybody can do it. The key to the universe turns out to be not some shattering revelation, but something which a lot of decent people do anyway, with scarcely a thought. Eternity lies not in a grain of sand but in a glass of water. The cosmos revolves on comforting the sick. When you act in this way, you are sharing in the love which built the stars. To live in this way is not just to have life, but to have it in abundance" (pp. 94–95).

[5] Our God-given tasks are themselves meant to give us life. See, for example, J. Richard Middleton, "From Primal Harmony to a Broken World: Distinguishing God's Intent for Life from the Encroachment of Death in Genesis 2–3," in *Earnest: Interdisciplinary Work Inspired by the Life and Teachings of B. T. Roberts*, eds. Andrew C. Koehl and David Basinger (Eugene, OR: Pickwick, 2017).

[6] See Fretheim, *God and World,* ch. 1, sec. titled "A Relational Creator and a Relational World."

[7] In ch. 4 ("Life in the Spirit"), I explore this in the context of *creation,* which is most relevant to my point here. For this theme in the context of *redemption,* see, for example, Margaret S. Archer, Andrew Collier, and Douglas V. Porpora, "What Do We Mean by God?" in *Transcendence: Critical Realism and God* (New York: Routledge, 2004), 39: "The work of God in this world – a work that involves human agents – is in the first place a work of undoing this alienation [between God and his creatures] by making God's presence manifest in all things. But we can go further and say that it is the purpose of God, without abolishing the distinction between God and creatures, to take up these creatures into God's own self so that they can participate in the divine nature and God can be all in all. To join in this work is the highest goal of humankind. It involves in the first place our own union with God; but it also involves the redemption of creation." And in the context of *eschatology* (or *the life of the age to come*), see, for example, Brenda B. Colijn, *Images of Salvation in the New Testament* (Downers Grove: IVP Academic, 2010), ch. 4: "Eternal life is the eschatological gift of God, the life of the kingdom of God in the age to come. It is everlasting life. More importantly, it has the qualities of joy and completeness that characterize the life of God. In fact, it *is* the life of God mediated to human beings by the Son of God and generated in them by the Spirit of God... Those who come to know Jesus begin to experience a life that is shaped and sustained by the love of God in

Christ. This life cannot be touched by death, and it will be perfected in the resurrection" (p. 99).

[8] Notice that "when Adam had lived 130 years, he had a son *in his own likeness, in his own image;* and he named him Seth" (Gen 5:3). As you can see in this text, the language of "image" and "likeness" seems to refer primarily to *offspring* (or "sonship"), at least *in the text,* before we compare it to the ancient Near Eastern literature it echoes and possibly subverts. Now, there's more to the meaning of God's image, but given the usage of "image" and "likeness" language by the biblical authors *in the whole of Scripture,* the sense of *offspring* seems to me primary. I think the sense of "ruling" over creation on God's behalf (which can be inferred from the context in Genesis 1:26–28: "so that they may rule...") is *part* of being children of God—it's our primary *role.* Our *identity,* however, is that of *sons and daughters of God.* Validating this view is Luke's genealogy of Jesus going all the way back to "Seth, the son of *Adam, the son of God"* (Luke 3:23b, 38). This confirms that humans are indeed children of God—or, at least, that we're meant to be. See also Paul, speaking to the Athenians at the Areopagus: "As some of your own poets have said, 'We are his offspring'" (Acts 17:28). He then goes on to use precisely "image" and "likeness" terminology: "Therefore since we are God's offspring, we should not think that the divine being is *like* gold or silver or stone—an *image* made by human design and skill" (v. 29). For a long time, I thought I was alone in noticing this as the primary meaning of God's "image" and "likeness" in Scripture, until I ran into Brian Rosner's discussion of the subject, in his *Known by God: A Biblical Theology of Personal Identity* (Grand Rapids: Zondervan Academic, 2017), p. 80ff: "In recent years a number of scholars have written in support of understanding the image of God in terms of sonship" (p. 82, n. 7). His list includes, Henri Blocher, *In the Beginning: The Opening Chapters of Genesis* (Leicester, UK: InterVarsity Press, 1984), p. 89; Peter J. Gentry and Stephen J. Wellum, *Kingdom through Covenant: A Biblical-Theological Understanding of the Covenants* (Wheaton: Crossway, 2012), pp. 28–29; John Dickson, *A Doubter's Guide to the Bible: Inside History's Bestseller for Believers and Skeptics* (Grand Rapids: Zondervan, 2014), p. 28; G. K. Beale, *A New Testament Biblical Theology: The Unfolding of the Old Testament in the New* (Grand Rapids: Baker Academic, 2011), p. 401; Gavin Ortlund, "Image of Adam, Son of God: Genesis 5:3 and Luke 3:38 in Intercanonical Dialogue," *Journal of the Evangelical Theological Society* 57, no. 4 (December 2014): pp. 679, 687; Graeme Goldsworthy, *The Son of God and the New Creation,* eds. Dane C. Ortlund and Miles V. Van Pelt, Short Studies in Biblical Theology (Wheaton: Crossway, 2015), pp. 61, 67; and Michael Horton, *The Christian Faith: A Systematic Theology for Pilgrims on the Way* (Grand Rapids: Zondervan, 2011), p. 388. See also Brian

S. Rosner, "Son of God at the Centre: Anthropology in Biblical-Theological Perspective," in *Anthropology and New Testament Theology*, eds. Jason Maston and Benjamin E. Reynolds (London: T&T Clark, 2018).

[9] Raymond C. Van Leeuwen, "Cosmos, Temple, House: Building and Wisdom in Ancient Mesopotamia and Israel," in *From the Foundations to the Crenellations: Essays on Temple Building in the Ancient Near East and Hebrew Bible*, eds. Mark J. Boda and Jamie Novotny, Alter Orient und Altes Testament 366 (Münster: Ugarit-Verlag, 2010), pp. 399–421; Watts, "The New Exodus/New Creational Restoration of the Image of God;" and G. K. Beale and Mitchell Kim, *God Dwells Among Us: Expanding Eden to the Ends of the Earth* (Downers Grove: InterVarsity Press, 2014).

[10] I am discovering precedent to this aspect of my project in Scandinavian creation theology: Niels Henrik Gregersen, Bengt Kristensson Uggla, and Trygve Wyller, eds., *Reformation Theology for a Post-Secular Age: Logstrup, Prenter, Wingren, and the Future of Scandinavian Creation Theology* (Göttingen: Vandenhoeck & Ruprecht, 2017); Gustaf Wingren, *Creation and Law*, repr. ed. (Eugene, OR: Wipf and Stock, 2003); Knud Eiler Logstrup, *The Ethical Demand*, eds. Hans Fink and Alasdair MacIntyre, repr. ed. (Notre Dame: University of Notre Dame Press, 1997); and in the following sources: J. Richard Middleton: *A New Heaven and a New Earth*, ch. 2: "Why Are We Here?: Being Human as Sacred Calling;" Middleton, "From Primal Harmony to a Broken World;" Middleton, "Creation Founded in Love: Breaking Rhetorical Expectations in Genesis 1:1–2:3," in *Sacred Text, Secular Times: The Hebrew Bible in the Modern World*, ed. Leonard Jay Greenspoon and Bryan F. LeBeau (Omaha, NE: Creighton University Press, 2000); Middleton, "A Sacred Calling for Sacred Work," Making All Things New conference, Center for Faith & Work, Redeemer Presbyterian Church, New York City. November 8, 2014, video of lecture, 30:37, https://vimeo.com/118729385; Terence E. Fretheim, *God and World*; Rikk E. Watts, "The New Exodus/New Creational Restoration of the Image of God;" pp. 15–41; William P. Brown, *The Seven Pillars of Creation: The Bible, Science, and the Ecology of Wonder* (New York: Oxford University Press, 2010); Brown, *The Ethos of the Cosmos: The Genesis of Moral Imagination in the Bible* (Grand Rapids: Wm. B. Eerdmans Publishing, 1999); Brown, *Sacred Sense: Discovering the Wonder of God's Word and World* (Grand Rapids: Wm. B. Eerdmans Publishing, 2015); Charles H. H. Scobie, *The Ways of Our God: An Approach to Biblical Theology* (Grand Rapids: Wm. B. Eerdmans, 2002), ch. 20, under "The Land of the Living," Kindle ed. There are weaknesses in Scobie's approach though, as pointed out by Ben Witherington: "A flat reading of the Bible, for instance a topical reading that largely ignores contexts and *developments* and mainly slots material from both the OT

and the NT into some abstract grid of 'themes' (see e.g. C. H. H. Scobie) does not do justice to the clues in the NT itself that we must read the canon *progressively.*" Ben Witherington III, *Biblical Theology: The Convergence of the Canon* (New York: Cambridge University Press, 2019), p. 3. I would agree that his approach has serious limitations, but I think he got the point of it all nonetheless.

[11] Brian J. Walsh and J. Richard Middleton, *The Transforming Vision: Shaping a Christian World View* (Downers Grove: IVP Academic, 1984), p. 44.

[12] Fretheim, *God and World*, p. xiv.

[13] See, for example, ibid, ch. 8: "Nature's Praise of God."

[14] Gustaf Wingren, *Creation and Law*, pp. 20–21.

[15] These statements are actually the subject of an old debate, one I still haven't fully engaged. At this point, consider my position just an intuition. But by what I've read so far on this, my sense is I will find enough support for it in other sources to validate it, though probably not without important qualifications. I'm exploring this concept within the context of Natural Theology. See, for example, Alister E. McGrath, *Re-Imagining Nature: The Promise of a Christian Natural Theology* (Chichester, West Sussex: John Wiley & Sons, 2017), p. 20: "Natural theology is the intellectual outcome of the natural tendency of the human mind to desire or be inclined toward God. This approach traditionally makes an appeal to the 'natural desire to see God,' developed by Thomas Aquinas, although more recent developments in the cognitive science of religion have opened up alternative ways of developing this theme. Other theologians have developed this notion in important ways – most notably, Bernard Lonergan's reformulation of this principle as an innate tendency of the human intellect, equivalent to the unrestricted desire to understand being." See also N. T. Wright, *History and Eschatology: Jesus and the Promise of Natural Theology* (Waco, TX: Baylor University Press, 2019); William P. Alston, *Perceiving God: The Epistemology of Religious Experience* (Ithaca, NY: Cornell University Press, 1993); and Richard Swinburne, *The Existence of God*, 2nd ed. (New York: Clarendon Press, 2004).

[16] J. Gordon McConville, *Being Human in God's World: An Old Testament Theology of Humanity* (Grand Rapids: Baker Academic, 2016), p. 172.

[17] David F Ford, *The Drama of Living: Becoming Wise in the Spirit* (London, UK: Canterbury Press Norwich, 2014), p. 53ff.

[18] Quoted by Ford, *The Drama of Living,* p. 57ff.

[19] David H. Kelsey, *Eccentric Existence: A Theological Anthropology,* 2 vols. (Louisville, KY: Westminster John Knox Press, 2009).

[20] Peter L. Berger and Thomas Luckmann, *The Social Construction of Reality: A Treatise in the Sociology of Knowledge* (New York: Anchor, 1967), p. 19.

[21] José Soto, "Inhabiting Reality," Wayfinders, June 12, 2021, https://www.wayfinders.quest/inhabiting-reality.html.

[22] We'll come back to the problem of otherworldly hope (or Christian *dualism)* in ch. 5. For a helpful introduction to the problem and history of dualism, see Walsh and Middleton, *The Transforming Vision,* chs. 6 and 7. See also Middleton, *A New Heaven and a New Earth,* ch. 1: "Introduction: The Problem of Otherworldly Hope;" George Eldon Ladd, *The Pattern of New Testament Truth* (Grand Rapids: Wm. B. Eerdmans Publishing, 1968), ch. 1: "The Background of the Pattern: Greek or Hebrew?" and Os Guinness, *The Call: Finding and Fulfilling the Central Purpose of Your Life* (Nashville: W. Publishing Group, 1998), ch. 4: "Everyone, Everywhere, Everything."

[23] See, for example, Richard Bauckham, *Gospel of Glory: Major Themes in Johannine Theology* (Grand Rapids: Baker Academic, 2015), p. 70.

[24] On the connection between God's intentions for the world and the good news of the gospel, see my reflections on "What Matters Most:" https://www.wayfinders.quest/what-matters-most.html.

CHAPTER 3
The Story of the Cross

This chapter began as a Scripture reflection I wrote some years ago for my church's website. The texts assigned to me truly captured the thrust of God's Story. And his Story, in turn, captured me.

I have a message from God in my heart concerning the sinfulness of the wicked.... Your love, LORD, reaches to the heavens, your faithfulness to the skies. Your righteousness is like the highest mountains, your justice like the great deep.... For with you is the fountain of life; in your light we see light. (Psalm 36)

Here is my servant, whom I uphold, my chosen one in whom I delight; I will put my Spirit on him, and he will bring justice to the nation.... I will keep you and will make you to be a covenant for the people and a light for the Gentiles.... See, the former things have taken place, and new things I declare; before they spring into being I announce them to you. (Isaiah 42:1–9)

On the first day of the Festival of Unleavened Bread, when it was customary to sacrifice the Passover lamb ... Jesus took bread ... "Take it; this is my body." Then he took a cup ... "This is my blood of the covenant, which is poured out for many." ... after I have risen, I will go ahead of you into Galilee.... My soul is overwhelmed with sorrow to the point of death.... Abba, Father, everything is possible for you. Take this cup from me. Yet not what I will, but what you will.... the Scriptures must be fulfilled.... "Are you the Messiah, the Son of the Blessed One?" "I am.... And you will see the Son

*of Man sitting at the right hand of the Mighty One and
coming on the clouds of heaven." ... Crucify him! ...
Why? What crime has he committed? ... Crucify him!
... And they crucified him.... It was nine in the morning
when they crucified him.... Let this Messiah, this king
of Israel, come down now from the cross, that we may
see and believe.... At noon, darkness came over the
whole land until three in the afternoon.... My God, my
God, why have you forsaken me? ... With a loud cry,
Jesus breathed his last.... The curtain of the temple
was torn in two from top to bottom.... "Surely this man
was the Son of God!"* (Mark 14–15)

In our Psalm we hear of God's commitment to his creatures,
despite the context of outright rebellion and wickedness in
which the psalmist speaks. Through Isaiah we learn that God
has something new up his sleeve, something about a covenant
through his "servant" who will be a light and bring justice to the
nations. In the Gospel it becomes clear who this Servant is; and
we learn, to our horror, that it's his own blood that will serve to
seal this new covenant.

So, what's God up to? What sort of story have we fallen into?[1]

God's Story and Ours
Our Story begins "In the beginning..." when the great "I AM"
said "Let there be..." to bring all things into existence (Gen 1).[2]

The Bible describes the cosmos as God's temple-palace,
his home, which he created with delight to inhabit with his
creatures.[3]

Then he created us, his children, in his own image and likeness
(Gen 1:26–28; 5:3; cf. Luke 3:23b, 38; Acts 17:28–2 9). He
breathed his life into us and crowned us with glory and honor

THE STORY OF THE CROSS

(Gen 2:7; cf. John 20:19, 21–22; Ps 8). He made us rulers and stewards of the earth, to care for and develop the rich potential he built into it. Just as he sits on the throne of his cosmic temple, so he has placed humanity as his vice-regents on the earth.[4]

But we rebelled against him (Gen 3). Satan lied to us about the possibility of God-like wisdom without God. About autonomy and freedom from God's authority. He said we would not die (as God had said we would) if we ate the forbidden fruit, questioning God's own heart. And he deceived us. Evil made its way to our hearts, and we betrayed our Maker.

Satan is not only a liar, he's the Accuser. That's what his name means. He wouldn't just deceive us so we would rebel. He would also make sure we suffer the consequences of our choices. So, the enemy's main weapons were twofold: temptation by *deception,* and *accusation* by appealing to God's justice.[5]

The Hero of Our Story
Astonishingly, God didn't give up on us, or his original plan to entrust the earth to us. In fact, the first thing he did when we went astray was to come and find us (Gen 3:8–9). And then he made garments for us, to cover our shame (v. 21). Our rebellion did have consequences (vv. 16–19). We were kicked out of the garden, and we surely died (vv. 22–24). But God, in his unsearchable wisdom, was going to find a way to restore us. Somehow humanity will continue to rule the earth under him, and with him, as his children.

So, just as in the beginning, he called a human being— Abraham—to go and bear his image, to be fruitful and multiply, in a new micro-cosmos—the promised land (Gen 12:1–3).

On the way there, this new humanity would receive God's instructions again—this time a full-fledged curriculum for life with God, as his children, worthy of his name (Deut 28; 30:19–20).

Through their life and mission, the rest of humanity could come to know God, and taste and see that he is good (Gen 18:18–19; Ps 34:8; Acts 3:25–26; Gal 3:8–9).

Rebellion persists here too (e.g., Ps 107). But God also persists (e.g., Isa 42:6; 49:6; 52:10; 60:3). And his final solution would show the depths of his commitment to us, the depths of his wisdom, and the depths of his mercy.[6]

God's final solution would be fit to meet the challenge we were facing. And this was our predicament. We had bought a lie, and now were entangled in lies, blind to the true nature of things. Our sins became deeply ingrained, forming sinful tendencies we couldn't shake (Isa 59:3–11; Rom 3:13–18; Titus 1:15). Deception and sin became part of the fabric of culture and society. And we stood condemned. The Accuser made sure we did.

But here's what the LORD had up his sleeve: He himself would take on the challenge. The Creator of the heavens and the earth would show up in human history, *as one of us,* to show us how it's done, to give us new precedents—a new Adam beginning a new humanity (Rom 5:12–18)—effectively re-writing our Story, re-forming Israel around himself, and doing what no one would have guessed he would do: to take on the Accuser by quietly sneaking into our Story *as the Accused* (cf. 1 Cor 2:7–8).

The Logic of the Story
What happened on the cross was earth-shaking. It didn't fit existing categories, the current economy of sinful humanity reaping the consequences of Sin in the world. This was no sinful human being that the powers were nailing to that cross. This was the righteousness of God incarnate. And it would cost the Satan dearly.

Here's the internal logic—the plot structure—of the biblical story as I understand it.[7] The LORD's Servant was representing

Israel, who was in turn representing humanity, who was in turn representing God on the earth. Humanity's plight was being addressed through Israel. And Israel's plight was being addressed through God's Servant. The LORD's final solution was to become the Servant himself. God himself would represent Israel. Which means that God himself would represent humanity. Humanity was destined for destruction, condemned for its betrayal and its wickedness. And it went to its destruction, condemned, on a cross.

We lived to tell the tale because our God—the one whom we betrayed, the one whose rules we broke—he made sure to sneak into the story Someone worthy to represent us on that cross. And only he—the One whose justice the Accuser appealed to—only he could take that responsibility, and take the full blow for us all. And he did. On that cross, humanity paid the penalty for its sins in full. And now the Accuser stands disarmed, forever (Col 2:13–15; Rev 12:10–11).

It's as the LORD had said: *"I am going to bring my servant, the Branch ... and I will remove the sin of this land in a single day"* (Zec 3:8–9; cf. Isa 52:13–53:12; Rom 8:1–4).

If we are in Christ, the worst the enemy can do now is to deceive us. *"But thanks be to God that, though you used to be slaves to sin, you have come to obey from your heart the pattern of teaching that has now claimed your allegiance. You have been set free from sin and have become slaves to righteousness"* (Rom 6: 17–18; cf. Phil 2:1–11; Ps 32:1–2).

Because the Lord paid the price, and the curtain of the temple split in two (Luke 23:44–46), our Father would burst out of his house, running with tears of joy to embrace those coming home: those who had been lost, now finally found (forgiven). And if he clothed Adam and Eve—still in Sin—to cover their shame, how much more will he now dignify us and crown us with glory and honor, as his own (cf. Luke 15)?

You are worthy to take the scroll
and to open its seals,
because you were slain,
and with your blood you purchased for God
persons from every tribe and language
and people and nation.
You have made them to be a kingdom
and priests to serve our God,
and they will reign on the earth.
(Rev 5:9–10; 21:3–5)

This is our Story. This is our God. May our lives reflect reality. The world needs it.

Whatever happens though, however grim things might look, let's remember the depths of his commitment to us, the depths of his wisdom, and the depths of his mercy. He's got this.

---

[1] To paraphrase Sam the Hobbit in J. R. R. Tolkien, *The Two Towers: Being the Second Part of the Lord of the Rings*, 2nd ed. (Boston, MA: Houghton Mifflin Company, 1982), p. 321. Besides the sources I'll mention later, I also found these sources helpful: Fleming Rutledge, *The Crucifixion: Understanding the Death of Jesus Christ* (Grand Rapids: Wm. B. Eerdmans Publishing, 2015); and Adam J. Johnson, *The Reconciling Wisdom of God: Reframing the Doctrine of the Atonement* (Bellingham: Lexham Press, 2016). Before I revised the final draft, I also read N. T. Wright, *The Day the Revolution Began: Reconsidering the Meaning of Jesus's Crucifixion* (San Francisco: HarperOne, 2016) to see how I was doing. It was encouraging to see that we seemed very much on the same page. It had been a while since I read anything by Wright, but I had followed his work for years.

[2] Here's a glimpse at the majesty of his masterpiece: https://vimeo.com/124910609.

[3] On the cosmos as God's home, see especially Raymond C. Van Leeuwen, "Cosmos, Temple, House: Building and Wisdom in Ancient Mesopotamia and Israel," in *From the Foundations to the Crenellations: Essays on Temple Building in the Ancient Near East and Hebrew Bible*, eds. Mark J. Boda and Jamie Novotny, Alter Orient Und Altes Testament 366 (Münster: Ugarit-Verlag, 2010), pp. 399–421; and Rikk E. Watts, "The New Exodus/New Creational Restoration of the Image of God," in *What Does It Mean to Be Saved? Broadening Evangelical Horizons of Salvation*, ed. John G. Stackhouse Jr. (Grand Rapids: Baker Academic, 2002), esp. pp. 18–23.

[4] For the connections I'm making here regarding the "image of God," I am indebted to Rikk E. Watts, "The New Exodus/New Creational Restoration of the Image of God." For a fuller explanation of my understanding of the meaning of the "image" and "likeness" of God in Scripture, see ch. 2 (n. 8), and ch. 4, sub-section "Life in the Spirit."

[5] For the connections I'm making regarding the *Satan* and what happened on the cross, see Henri Blocher, "Agnus Victor: The Atonement as Victory and Vicarious Punishment," in *What Does It Mean to Be Saved?* ed. John G. Stackhouse Jr., pp. 67–91. See also my initial exploration of the connection between the serpent in Genesis 3 and the *Satan* figure we find in the rest of the Scriptures: https://www.wayfinders.quest/on-the-satan.html.

[6] Here's a glimpse at our Father's heart: https://vimeo.com/129675222.

[7] The insight on the "plot structure" of the biblical story is from Richard Middleton, *A New Heaven and a New Earth: Reclaiming Biblical Eschatology* (Grand Rapids: Baker Academic, 2014), ch. 3: "The Plot of the Biblical Story."

CHAPTER 4
Life in the Spirit

Have you ever heard a presentation of the gospel in which the coming of the Spirit of God was central? I just did, by the apostle Paul.

> *He redeemed us in order that the blessing given to Abraham might come to the Gentiles through Christ Jesus, so that by faith we might receive the promise of the Spirit.* (Gal 3:14)

The Gospel

In what follows, we'll explore the significance of this "promise of the Spirit" to the apostolic gospel, which will shed surprising light on the nature of the Story we're trying to inhabit. This will take us for a significant ride through the narrative-world of the Bible, but it will lead to the very heart of Christian discipleship, and to the ultimate meaning of life itself.[1]

The Blessing and the Promise

Before we explore the "promise of the Spirit," let's try to unpack the content of the "blessing given to Abraham," since they seem to be related.

God's blessing to Abraham came in the form of promises: promises of land (Gen 12:1, 7; 13:14–17; 15:7, 18–19; 17:8; 22:17; 26:3–4; 28:4, 13; 35:12), descendants (12:2; 13:16; 15:5; 17:4–6; 22:17; 26:4, 24; 28:3, 14; 35:11), a great reputation (12:2), God's protection (12:3), and the promise of *blessing* itself (12:2–3a; 17:1–8; 22:17)—not just for him and his family, but that through him "all peoples on earth will be blessed" (12:3b; 12:2b NRSV; 18:18–19; cf. Acts 3:25–26; Gal 3:8–9).

To understand what "blessing" itself is about, a good place to start is Deuteronomy 30:19, where Moses pretty much equates "blessings" with *life,* just as he equates "curses" with *death* (cf. Ps 133). "Blessing," in this general sense, is basically *all that we need to thrive,* which is why God showered us with it at creation, through both words and actions (Gen 1:1–2:4a).[2]

To "bless" is both what God does and what his people do as his agents in the world: he promises to bless the children of Abraham, and also commissions them to be a blessing to the rest of the world. It's how God is blessing all the families of the earth, *through his people* (e.g., Gen 12:3b; 18:18–19; Gal 3:14). We'll come back to this in a moment.[3]

In terms of God's part, his blessing is all that we need *from him* in order to flourish. It's the approval, validation, favor, provision and protection of our Creator who says: *Go and be what I created you to be: live, be fruitful, and thrive* (e.g., Gen 1; Isa 65:23; Ezek 34:26; Mal 3:12). This definition helps explain why "blessing" can sum up all that God promised Abraham.[4]

The Calling
Now, even though in his kindness God gives good things to all his creatures (Matt 5:45; Ps 104; Acts 14:15–17), his blessing rightly begins with being on good terms with the One who's blessing us (e.g., Ps 1; 32:1–2; 112:1–2; Jer 17:7)—that relationship itself being the ultimate blessing: to be children of God and part of his family.[5]

But if we have been reading the biblical story up to that point in Genesis 12, when God called Abraham, we know that all the families of the earth had decidedly *not* been on good terms with God. And Abraham was called precisely to remedy that.[6] He was called to walk in God's ways, in order to be a witness to the goodness of God and of his ways (e.g., Gen 18:18–19). To the reality that only in God's ways will we find the life that we're made for, and the blessings we need.

The problem was that the children of Abraham—placed right in the center of the known world, in order to be a light to the rest of the world—were themselves not able to walk in God's ways, and thus failed to provide the witness the nations needed. Rather than find life in God's ways, Israel was itself reaping the "curse of the Law" (cf. Gal 3:13), the "death" about which Moses warned them if they didn't walk in God's ways.

> *This day I call the heavens and the earth as witnesses against you that I have set before you life and death, blessings and curses. Now choose life, so that you and your children may live and that you may love the LORD your God, listen to his voice, and hold fast to him. For the LORD is your life, and he will give you many years in the land he swore to give to your fathers, Abraham, Isaac and Jacob.* (Deut 30:19–20; cf. Deut 28)

The rest is history. The most striking feature of the Old Testament narrative is all the ups and downs of the people of God: their going astray and paying the consequences, followed by repentance and God's rescue, again and again (e.g., Ps 107). And it's why the Son of God had to come from God to make a way where there clearly was no way: if left up to us, it just wasn't going to happen.[7]

And so, just as God sent Israel for the sake of the world, so he sent his Son for the sake of Israel (Matt 15:24). "Christ redeemed us from the curse of the law by becoming a curse for us, for it is written: 'Cursed is everyone who is hung on a pole'" (Gal 3:13 citing Deut 21:23).

But wait, "redeemed" who? Well, Israel, first of all, to set them free to be the *light to the nations* they were called to be (Isa 42:6; 49:6; 52:10; 60:3; John 8:12; Acts 13:47; 26:23). And that's exactly what we got when twelve apostles representing the twelve tribes of Israel went and did what the Lord had sent them to do (Matt 28:19–20; Luke 24:45–50; Acts 1:4–5), "in order that the blessing given to Abraham might come to the Gentiles through Christ Jesus, so that by faith we might receive the promise of the Spirit." (Gal 3:14; cf. Luke 24:49).[8]

The Promise of the Spirit

Now, when we go to the Old Testament in search of this "promise of the Spirit" (Gal 3:14; Eph 1:13–14), we actually find no explicit promise of the Spirit from God to Abraham. What we do find is the development of a sense of expectation for the coming of the Spirit as part of the fulfilment of God's promises in general, including his promises to Abraham. This is true in two main senses: one general and implicit, the other specific and explicit.

Echoes of God's Promise

First, there's a general sense of expectation that God would act again through his Spirit, as he had in the past. As we'll see below, God has a tendency to act in his creation through his Spirit, both as creator and as redeemer, so that the coming of the Spirit is expected as part of the fulfillment of God's promises in general.

But there's also a specific promise of the Spirit which is part of the promised *new covenant,* when God will give his people *new hearts* through his Spirit (Ezek 36:26–27). This isn't the only time God explicitly promises the Spirit in the Old Testament (I'll mention others later), but it's probably the most significant one (cf. Rom 2:29; Heb 8), and it's likely one Paul has in mind in his reference to "the promise of the Spirit."

The LORD your God will circumcise your hearts and the hearts of your descendants, so that you may love him with all your heart and with all your soul, and live. (Deut 30:6—a promise echoed through Jeremiah in terms of a new covenant)

"This is the covenant I will make with the people of Israel after that time," declares the LORD. "I will put my law in their minds and write it on their hearts. I will be their God, and they will be my people. No longer will they teach their neighbor, or say to one another, 'Know the LORD,' because they will all know me, from the least of them to the greatest," declares the LORD. "For I will forgive their wickedness and will remember their sins no more." (Jer 31:33–34—later echoed through Ezekiel in terms of the work of the Spirit)

I will give you a new heart and put a new spirit in you; I will remove from you your heart of stone and give you a heart of flesh. And I will put my Spirit in you and move you to follow my decrees and be careful to keep my laws. (Ezek 36:26–27)

These are the texts behind Romans 2:29: *"a person is a Jew who is one inwardly; and circumcision is circumcision of the heart, by the Spirit, not by the written code."* So, when Paul speaks of "the promise of the Spirit" in Galatians and Ephesians, this sense of the promise is at least part of what he has in mind.

What I'm suggesting, then, is that Paul probably has more than one sense of the promise in mind. In fact, he could have *both* the general sense of expectation for the coming of the Spirit, and *multiple* particular referents to the promise in mind.

For example, besides the general sense of expectation for the coming of the Spirit, he could have the *new covenant* in mind (as he does in Romans 2:29), *and* he could also be reading back-ward, reasoning back to Genesis from his own experience of what God was doing in the church through the Spirit:

> Paul could readily deduce that, through the giving of the Spirit, God was making Abraham the father of in-numerable descendants [as he promised in Genesis 22:17]—of all those who, through baptism, were be-ing incorporated into Christ, the Seed of Abraham"
> —David A. deSilva[9]

If this is so, then Paul is reading Genesis in light of the rest of the Story, and finding the promise of the Spirit implicit in prom-ises made to Abraham.

God's Story and His Spirit

In any case, these expectations regarding "the promise of the Spirit" are best understood within the larger Story the Scriptures are telling: a story that began at creation and will end in a new creation—both brought about through the Spirit.[10]

That Story begins in Genesis 1, when God's Spirit hovered over primordial waters at the beginning of creation (Gen 1:2). Al-though the Spirit is only mentioned one time in Genesis 1, the overall sense in the Scriptures is that this Spirit "hovering over the waters" was involved in God's creative work. God also cre-ated the world by his *word,* a word that is itself associated with his Spirit, since the Hebrew word for Spirit *(rûaḥ)* also means *breath* and *wind:* God's Spirit *is* his breath. "By the word of the LORD the heavens were made, their starry host by the breath of his mouth" (Ps 33:6). "When you send your Spirit, they are created, and you renew the face of the ground" (Ps 104:30).[11]

We see God's *rûaḥ* again during the flood, in Genesis 8:1, when God "sent a *wind [rûaḥ]* over the earth, and the waters receded." While in Genesis 1 God brought order to creation through his *rûaḥ* "hovering over the waters," during the flood he sends his *rûaḥ* once again to subdue the waters and begin a new creation.

Later on (in Exodus 14:21), as Pharaoh's army pursued Israel, "Moses stretched out his hand over the sea, and all that night the LORD drove the sea back with a strong east *wind [rûaḥ]* and turned it into dry land." If it wasn't for the poem that followed, however, we might have missed something of the nature of this "strong east wind."

> *By the blast of your nostrils*
> the waters piled up.
> The surging waters stood up like a wall...
> The enemy boasted,
> 'I will pursue, I will overtake...
> I will gorge myself on them...'
> *But you blew with your breath,*
> and the sea covered them.
> (Exod 15:8–10)

Can you see the pattern that's beginning to emerge? It is through his *rûaḥ* that God tends to act, work, and come to the rescue when his people need help. At least, that's what we're coming to expect by this point in the story.

> The Torah [from Genesis to Deuteronomy] sets a pattern regarding the *rûaḥ* acting to fulfil God's creational purposes. The *rûaḥ* brings order to the watery unformed creation (Gen. 1:2) and acts to master waters in order to fulfil God's plans in establishing a righteous 'new humanity' with Noah's offspring (Gen. 8:1) and Abraham's seed (Exod. 14:21; 15:8, 10). With the drama of God's redemption of creation just beginning to unfold in the Torah, a reader wonders whether God's *rûaḥ* will again act to further fulfil his promises of cosmic redemption. —VanGemeren and Abernethy[12]

Which he will, beginning by empowering people to lead Israel and bring order to society. This can be said explicitly of Joseph (Gen 41:38), then of Moses (Num 11:17)—whose legacy would continue later in the ministry of the prophets (Deut 18:15–18; Mal 4:4),[13] then of those who built the Tabernacle (Exod 31:1–7; 35:30–35), of the seventy elders (Num 11:25), and of Joshua (27:18)—though Moses wished God put his *rûaḥ* on all his people (11:29), a wish that would be granted soon enough (Acts 2:14–21; cf. Joel 2:28–32).

In the time of the Judges, we see God's *rûaḥ* empowering Othniel (Judg 3:10), Gideon (6:34), Jephthah (11:29), and Samson (13:25; 14:6, 19; 15:14, 19). However, if you've read the book of Judges, you know that despite God's interventions, all is *not* well during this period: "In those days Israel had no king; everyone did as they saw fit" (Judg 17:6; 21:25, etc.). But while Judges ends "hoping for a king who would rule under God's Lordship, Samuel presents David as a ray of light awaiting the dawn of an anointed king who would reign justly and in the fear of the Lord without faltering" (VanGemeren and Abernethy).[14]

> *These are the last words of David ... "The Spirit of the LORD spoke through me; his word was on my tongue. The God of Israel spoke, the Rock of Israel said to me: 'When one rules over people in righteousness, when he rules in the fear of God, he is like the light of morning at sunrise on a cloudless morning, like the brightness after rain that brings grass from the earth.'"* (2 Sam 23:1–4)

Sadly, David didn't live up to the Spirit's desires (2 Sam 11–12), and neither did most of his sons. Yet, the LORD had promised to David:

> *Once for all, I have sworn by my holiness—
> and I will not lie to David—*

that his line will continue forever
and his throne endure before me like the sun;
it will be established forever like the moon,
the faithful witness in the sky.
(Ps 89: 35–37)

So there arose the expectation, based on these promises, of a coming righteous king from the line of David—a Messiah, God's Anointed One:

A shoot will come up from the stump of Jesse [David's dad];
from his roots a Branch will bear fruit.
The Spirit of the LORD will rest on him—
the Spirit of wisdom and of understanding,
the Spirit of counsel and of might,
the Spirit of the knowledge and fear of the LORD—
and he will delight in the fear of the LORD.
(Isa 11:1–3; cf. 42:1–4; 61:1–3)

But it wasn't just leaders, prophets and Messiah whom the Spirit would empower. Eventually, God would pour out his Spirit on "all people" (Joel 2:28, cf. Num 11:29)—even on the land itself (Isa 32:15–18; 44:3)—to bring about a new creation (Isa 28–35), when even the dead will rise from their graves (Ezek 37:1–14).[15]

These expectations help explain why the events the apostles witnessed happened "in accordance with the Scriptures" (e.g., Matt 1:22–23; 1 Cor 15:3–4; Acts 2:16): the restoration the Lord was bringing about (Luke 3:22; 4:18–19; Acts 10:38), the democratization of the gift of prophecy (Acts 2:14–21), even the resurrection itself (Mark 12:18–27; 16:1–7; Rom 8:21–25; 2 Cor 5:1–5)—these were all "promises of the Spirit!"

The Logic of the Story

Of course, as we keep reading our Story in the New Testament, and then in church history, we learn that the fulfilment of this promised restoration turned out to be *a process*—not a *once and for all* kind of event, as we might have hoped.[16] The same can be said about the coming of *God's kingdom,* which includes this promised restoration: all authority in heaven and on earth has *already* been given to the Son of God (Matt 28:18), but his will is still *not* done without opposition.

The reason why it had to be this way, it seems to me, is because God hasn't given up on his original intention to rule the earth *through us* (Gen 1:26–27). That's why this is taking time! And it's why at the heart of this "promise" was the solution to the root of all our problems: the transformation of *our hearts,* the *ability* to walk in God's ways that we might live and thrive as our Creator has longed to see from the beginning (Gen 1:28).[17]

So, the Lord Jesus paid the ransom that set us *free* from "our legal indebtedness" (Col 2:13–15; cf. Rev 12:10–11), and by the coming of the Spirit we're actually *enabled* to live out that freedom: "the freedom and glory of the children of God" (Rom 8:21).[18]

This, then, is the content of the apostolic gospel: that the promise made to Abraham regarding the blessing of the nations—a blessing that includes all of the above—had finally begun to be fulfilled. The coming of the Spirit was evidence of that (Acts 2; 10:34–48). "Scripture foresaw that God would justify the Gentiles by faith, and announced the gospel in advance to Abraham: 'All nations will be blessed through you'" (Gal 3:8).[19]

God with Us

As we know, the promise of the Spirit was formally fulfilled on the day of Pentecost (Acts 2; cf. Luke 24:49), when the Holy Spirit came and filled the church with the Presence of God.

That's right, with the Presence of God. The Spirit we received at Pentecost was the same "Presence" that took Israel out of Egypt and led them through the wilderness (Isa 63:9–14).[20] The Spirit of God = the Presence of God = God himself!

As we'll see below, what happened at Pentecost was basically the coming of Emmanuel all over again, and in a new way. A coming that had precedent not only in the Incarnation of the Son of God, but also in the expectation of the coming of Yahweh in the Old Testament.

> Paul thus regularly spoke of the spirit in ways which indicate that he regarded the spirit, as he regarded the Messiah, as the glorious manifestation of YHWH himself. This conclusion is not dependent on one or two verbal echoes, but relies on the regular and repeated invocation of the various elements of the foundational exodus-narrative. The spirit is, it seems, the ultimate mode of YHWH's personal and powerful presence with, and even in, his people. —N. T. Wright and Michael F. Bird[21]

God's coming (or returning) has always been at the heart of the good news we longed to hear, and the one we finally heard. Everything else we needed would follow, as expected when Father comes home. It was the same when his Son came too, because *when we see the Son, we see the Father* (John 14:8–11). And it turns out that something similar is going on with his Spirit too.[22]

To think that it was better for the Lord Jesus to leave us so that his Spirit would come (John 16:7–11)—what could possibly be better than face-to-face relationship with the Son of God? Well, it looks like the answer is *oneness with God.* But I get ahead of myself.

God's Empowering Presence

Gordon Fee points out the extent of the Spirit's involvement in the life of the believer, and of the church:

> ... the Thessalonians' conversion is by the sanctifying work of the Spirit (2 Thess 2:13; cf. 1 Cor 6:11; Rom 15:16), as is their accompanying joy (1 Thess 1:6; cf. Rom 15:13). Revelation comes through the Spirit (1 Cor 2:10; Eph 3:5); and Paul's preaching is accompanied by the power of the Spirit (1 Thess 1:5). Prophetic speech and speaking in tongues result directly from speaking by the Spirit (1 Cor 12:3; 14:2, 16). By the Spirit the Romans put to death any sinful practices (Rom 8:13). Paul desires the Ephesians to be strengthened by means of God's Spirit (Eph 3:16). Believers serve by the Spirit (Phil 3:3), love by the Spirit (Col 1:8), are sealed by the Spirit (Eph 1:13), and walk and live by the Spirit (Gal 5:16, 25). Finally, believers are "saved through washing by the Spirit, whom God poured out upon them" (Titus 3:5).[23]

Not only that, but...

> The Spirit searches all things (1 Cor 2:10), knows the mind of God (1 Cor 2:11), teaches the content of the gospel to believers (1 Cor 2:13), dwells among or within believers (1 Cor 3:16; Rom 8:11; 2 Tim 1:14), accomplishes all things (1 Cor 12:11), gives life to those who believe (2 Cor 3:6), cries out from within our hearts (Gal 4:6), leads us in the ways of God (Gal 5:18; Rom 8:14), bears witness with our own spirits (Rom 8:16), has desires that are in opposition to the flesh (Gal 5:17), helps us in our weakness (Rom 8:26), intercedes in our behalf (Rom 8:26–27), works all things together for our ultimate good (Rom 8:28),

strengthens believers (Eph 3:16), and is grieved by our sinfulness (Eph 4:30).[24]

And I am undone. Can you sense the nature of this relationship? The oneness? He's not only making his dwelling among us; he's making us one with himself (cf. 1 Cor 6:17). Do you see that? This is what he had promised: "On that day you will realize that I am in my Father, and you are in me, and I am in you" (John 14:20).

> 'That day' is the day when Jesus will have returned to the Father and sent the Spirit to be with and in his disciples. *Then they will learn in a new way the truth of his mutual oneness with the Father of which they had so often heard him speak.* They will know in their own experience that as he is in the Father they are in their living Lord and their living Lord in them. This threefold coinherence [or "mutual indwelling"] is a coinherence of love; those who are admitted to it are those who love their living Lord, showing their love by their obedience....
>
> The disciples, already loved by the Father and by the Son, now have the same Spirit imparted to them and, being introduced by him into the circle of the divine love, are enabled not only to reciprocate that love but also to manifest it to one another and to all mankind (cf. Rom. 5:5; 15, 30; Col. 1:8). —F. F. Bruce[25]

And so, an answer starts to emerge for me as to why it was better for the Lord to "leave us" so the Spirit would come. It's because he didn't *really* leave us! In fact, by the coming of the Spirit to make his home among us, and within us, all three (Father, Son and Spirit) are now with us in a new and more intimate way.

To be clear, all three are with us *in a sense,* because the Lord did leave in the sense that we don't see his resurrected body around these days. Nevertheless, given the evidence above, it seems clear to me that all three are with us *in a real sense.*

I take my cue from Philip's experience, when he asked the Lord to show him the Father (John 14:8–11). The Lord seemed perplexed by the question: *How could you ask that, Philip?* Listen to his response:

> Jesus answered: *"Don't you know me, Philip, even after I have been among you such a long time?* Anyone who has seen me has seen the Father. How can you say, 'Show us the Father'? Don't you believe that I am in the Father, and that the Father is in me?"

Who was it that answered Philip's question? Philip wants to see the Father and Jesus answers: *"Don't you know me, Philip?"* Can you hear the Father himself responding through the lips of Jesus?

Oneness with God

Let's come back to the question, then, about why it was better for the Lord Jesus to leave us so we could have the Spirit (John 15:26–16:15).

It was probably not because "the Spirit of truth" was better able to prove the world wrong about sin, righteousness and judgement (John 16:7–11; cf. v. 13). Nor because he's a better "Advocate" than the Son of God (cf. v. 7). They always work together. There is no Holy Spirit without the Son of God, and there's no Son of God without the Holy Spirit.

It was in the power of the Spirit that the Lord Jesus was born (Luke 1:35), and then did all he did when he came to our rescue (John 1:32–34; Luke 4:14, etc.; Rom 8:11). And it's from the

Son of God that the Spirit gets what he gives to us (John 16:14–15). There's that oneness again that so intrigues me. And it's why it was better that the Lord Jesus leave us so we could have the Spirit: because through the Spirit, *we* can join that oneness. So that what God is up to on earth can be accomplished *through us*.[26]

Now, clearly, the Son of God is unique in *his* oneness with God (e.g., Phil 2:6). In his eternal existence with the Father (e.g., John 1:1–4; 17:5; Col 1:15–20). But besides that, I see three main realities going on here, making such oneness possible and comprehensible, all now available to us through the Spirit.

Representing God, Not Ourselves

One is the reality and the logic of *representation* in the narrative-world of the Bible. I explored this in Chapter 3: "The LORD's Servant was representing Israel, who was in turn representing humanity, who was in turn representing God on the earth. Humanity's plight was being addressed through Israel. And Israel's plight was being addressed through God's Servant."[27]

Looking at it the other way around, the Lord Jesus was representing the Father (to Israel). And just as Moses is like God to Pharaoh (Exod 7:1–2), and the prophets' words are "the word of Yahweh" (cf. 2 Pet 1:21), so Jesus' words are the Father's words. When we see the Son, we see the Father, because he represents him. Likewise, *we* represent the Son and thus the Father. And when people bless or curse Jesus' followers, for example, they are blessing or cursing Jesus himself (e.g., Matt 25:37–40)—precisely because we're *his* representatives (e.g., 1 John 4:17 CEB, NRSV).

A similar dynamic is going on with humanity in general: believers or not, humans are God's representatives on earth (Gen 1:26–28). That was established at creation and still holds.

It is why God is giving us his Spirit, you see: to enable us to be and do what he's wanted us to be and do from the beginning.

Enacting God's Vision

The second aspect I see to this oneness is related to the first and it's a oneness of *agency*.[28] We hear the Lord Jesus say that he does nothing except what he sees the Father doing (John 5:15–23; 11:38; 14:8–11). I think such oneness of agency is our aim too as his followers.

We can see it at work in the apostles after Pentecost. In the book of Acts, we see the church "turning the world upside down" (in a good way), but you get the sense that it's really God himself making all the moves and running the show through his Spirit (Acts 17:6 NRSV). Paul, for example, can even say that it's no longer he who lives but Christ who lives in him (Gal 2:20). Now *that's* surrender. And oneness with God, as you can imagine, requires surrender.

Life in the Spirit

The third reality I see going on in this oneness is the subject of this discussion and what actually makes it happen: the real Presence of God with us, and in us, through his Spirit.

Now, to understand this idea of God's Spirit *indwelling* his people, we'll need to go back to the beginning of our Story, this time to the creation account of Genesis 2.

> *Then the Lord God formed a man from the dust of the ground and breathed into his nostrils the breath of life, and the man became a living being.* (Gen 2:7)

We have at least three reasons to believe that the "breath" of God in Genesis 2:7 (nišmat ḥayyîm) refers to the same reality that "the Spirit of God" does elsewhere in Scripture (e.g., Job 33:4; Ps 146:3–4).[29]

First, because the beginnings of Genesis 1 (1:1–3) and Genesis 2 (2:4b–7) are parallel texts (structurally)—one echoing the other—the "Spirit" of Genesis 1 and the "breath" of Genesis 2 can be taken as speaking about the same reality. Though that only makes sense because the Hebrew word for "Spirit" in Genesis 1 *(rûaḥ)* also means "breath," as I explained earlier.

The second reason is actually "behind" the text, in ancient Near Eastern parallels to what God was doing in Genesis 2:7. Let's take a quick look at that background to see what light it sheds on the meaning of God sharing his breath or Spirit with human beings. It is significant.

Old Testament scholar Richard Middleton explains that God's breathing the breath of life into the man in Genesis 2 bears many of the marks of an ancient Mesopotamian ritual known as "the opening of the mouth" or "the washing of the mouth."[30] This ritual "typically took place in a sacred grove beside a river (a motif echoed in the garden narrative in Genesis 2). The purpose of the ritual was to vivify the newly carved cult statue so that it would become a living entity, imbued with the spirit and presence of the deity for which it was an image."[31]

Middleton explains that "when Genesis 1 and 2 are read together against the background of ancient Near Eastern notions … humanity is understood as the authorized cult statue in the cosmic temple, *the decisive locus of divine presence on earth,* the living image of God in the cosmic sanctuary."[32]

All that we have learned about the gospel and the promise of the Spirit belongs in this larger picture of humanity as the image of God in his cosmic sanctuary. This is key to understanding the nature of reality according to the Scriptures, which is key to understanding the content of the gospel and why it is good news.[33]

The Bible describes the cosmos as God's temple-palace, his home and ours too.[34] That is the nature of creation. God made humans in his own "image" and "likeness" (Gen 1:26–27), which means that he made us *like him* in some sense, but also that we are to *image* him—to *be* like him—ruling over the earth on his behalf, and *as he would* (v. 26).

There seem to be various senses to the meaning of God's "image," but however one looks at it, being "the image of God" has to do with *representation*.[35] We're not just any image though, or any representative, we are *children of God.* That is the primary meaning of the "image" and "likeness" of God in Scripture (cf. Gen 5:3; Luke 3:23b, 38; Acts 17:28–29), a meaning that *includes* our ruling over the earth on our Father's behalf (Gen 1:26–28).[36] Genesis 2 then takes the ancient Near Eastern notion of a god's image being "imbued with the spirit and presence of the deity" and *legitimates it,* as also reflecting something of how God created *us.*[37]

Now, the typical climax of temple inauguration ceremonies, both in the Bible and in the ancient Near East, is when God or the gods *move into* their newly built home: either by the placing of the image in the temple of the god it represents, or by God's very Presence filling the tabernacle and the temple (Exod 40:34–35; 1 Kgs 8:6–11; 2 Chr 5; Ezra 43:1–5; Rev 21:1–4). But here's the thing: we don't see God's Presence filling the earth at the end of Genesis' creation accounts—which one would expect, if the cosmos is God's temple. And that's precisely the point of Genesis 1:26–28 and 2:7: *we* are to fill the earth with God's presence![38]

> It is imperative to understand what this means ... although we are self-conscious beings, our destiny lies not in an individualistic self-fulfillment or self-glorification but *in our conforming to the Other*—namely, the God in whose image we are made —Rikk E. Watts[39]

Of course, we did go astray in Genesis 3 and, well, the rest is history. But that's precisely what the Lord came to address. He came *to restore the image of God on earth* (1 Cor 15:21–22, 45–49; 2 Cor 3:18; Col 1:15), and he's still at it (Rom 5:9–11; 8:15–17; 1 Cor 1:8; 2 Cor 5:17; Gal 6:15).[40] It remains for us, then, to go and find out what this means—as we have been doing—because it seems pretty clear that the ball is in our court now. Such is the invitation of the gospel.

> *On the evening of that first day of the week, when the disciples were together, with the doors locked for fear of the Jewish leaders, Jesus came and stood among them and said, "Peace be with you! ... As the Father has sent me, I am sending you." And with that he breathed on them and said, "Receive the Holy Spirit."*
> (John 20:19, 21–22)

This, finally, is the third reason why we can equate the breath of God in Genesis 2:7 with God's Spirit. As Craig S. Keener writes, "Most scholars concur that when Jesus breathes on the disciples, John is alluding to the creative, life-imparting act of God in Gen 2:7; Jesus is creating a new humanity, a new creation."[41]

Now we have what it takes to be one with God—to be what he created us to be—to fill the earth with his Presence and his life![42] Of course, we only know in part what God is up to (1 Cor 13:9–12), so it's often not straightforward how one is to proceed or what to make of things—but we need to *trust* him.

The Holy Spirit knows the mind of God (1 Cor 2:11), knows absolutely all that's going on (1 Cor 2:10), and knows exactly how he's making all things new (cf. Isa 43:18–19; 2 Cor 5:17; Rev 21:15). He brings us into the flow of the life and the will of God (Gen 1:26–28; John 14:20; 16:12–15), gives us a role to play and makes us part of what he's doing (e.g., Gen 1:26–28; 7:1–5; 9:7–13; 12:1–3; Exod 3:1–10; Matt 28:18–20; Luke

4:18–19; 5:14; Gal 5:25; Phil 3:3; Col 1:8). How well we're able to play such a role hinges on how much we're able to yield to his Spirit (Rom 8:1–17; 1 Pet 4:11). On how much of ourselves we conform to the One in whose image we're made (Rom 8:14, 29; 2 Cor 3:18). The more we do, the more we realize how right this is—that it's just what we're made for.

Conclusion

We have come to the end of our journey here and have to wrap up. This I have learned: that if I'm ever looking for the heart of the gospel, it's got to be somewhere around this oneness we've been trying to understand. God himself living through a new humanity, through the Body of Christ, *that* is the life of the age to come. It has begun.[43]

God's Grandeur

The world is charged with the grandeur of God.
It will flame out, like shining from shook foil;
It gathers to a greatness, like the ooze of oil
Crushed. Why do men then now not reck his rod?
Generations have trod, have trod, have trod;
And all is seared with trade; bleared, smeared with toil;
And wears man's smudge and shares man's smell: the soil
Is bare now, nor can foot feel, being shod.

And for all this, nature is never spent;
There lives the dearest freshness deep down things;
And though the last lights off the black West went
Oh, morning, at the brown brink eastward, springs—
Because the Holy Ghost over the bent
World broods with warm breast and with ah! bright wings.

—Gerard Manley Hopkins[44]

[1] An earlier version of this essay was part of an independent study on the gospel completed at Northeastern Seminary. I'm sharing an online version of this discussion at https://www.wayfinders.quest/holy-spirit.html.

[2] And if there's any doubt about God's heart toward the work of his hands in Genesis 1, see J. Richard Middleton, "Creation Founded in Love: Breaking Rhetorical Expectations in Genesis 1:1–2:3," in *Sacred Text, Secular Times: The Hebrew Bible in the Modern World,* eds. Leonard Jay Greenspoon and Bryan F. LeBeau (Omaha, NE: Creighton University Press, 2000).

[3] Some biblical scholars reject a "missional" reading of Gen 12:1–3, arguing that the blessing promised there is mostly for the benefit of Abraham and his descendants, not that of the nations. I found Richard Middleton helpful here also, as he's argued convincingly against this position in "The Blessing of Abraham and the *Missio Dei:* Reframing the Purpose of Israel's Election in Genesis 12:1–3," in *Orthodoxy and Orthopraxy: Essays in Tribute to Paul Livermore,* eds. Douglas R. Cullum and J. Richard Middleton (Eugene, OR: Pickwick, 2020): "For a variety of reasons, then, we are warranted in viewing Abraham and his descendants as entrusted with the task of participating with God in the *missio Dei* to address (and overcome) the obstacle of sin among the nations, thus restoring the human race to its original purpose. That this is a *task* or *calling* given to Abraham, and not simply a promise of what God will unilaterally do, is suggested by the fact that the verb for 'be' a blessing at the end of Gen 12:2 is technically in the form of an imperative or command (thus, 'be a blessing!')," p. 58. See also Christopher J. H. Wright, *The Mission of God: Unlocking the Bible's Grand Narrative* (Downers Grove: IVP Academic, 2006).

[4] These statements and the treatment that follows on the meaning of these promises of "blessing" are largely my own synthesis of what I'm learning. Besides the secondary sources mentioned or quoted, I also consulted the following: Mary J. Evans, "Blessing/Curse," in *New Dictionary of Biblical Theology: Exploring the Unity Diversity of Scripture*, eds. Brian S. Rosner et al. (Downers Grove: IVP Academic, 2000), pp. 398–402; and T. Desmond Alexander, "Promises, Divine," in *Dictionary of the Old Testament: Pentateuch,* eds. T. Desmond Alexander and David W. Baker (Downers Grove: IVP Academic, 2002), pp. 656–62.

[5] In "Blessing/Curse," Mary J. Evans sees this as the *only* aspect of God's blessings that truly matters—or at least, so it seems: "NT teaching echoes the OT view of blessing and cursing as relational. The ultimate and only important blessing is that of belonging to God, being part of his people,

a member of his family. The only real curse is being out [of] relationship with God, outside of the community of blessing. In temporal contexts both blessings and curses can be described in material terms, but their material dimension is secondary" (p. 402). I agree that our relationship to God is the most important of his blessings, but to see it as the *only* important blessing makes it seem as if God isn't interested in the well-being and flourishing of his creatures *as an end in itself,* and I don't think that's the case.

[6] See Middleton, "The Blessing of Abraham and the *Missio Dei.*"

[7] I'm in the habit of reading the Old Testament as *our* story, as I take seriously the biblical claim that Christians are children of Abraham (e.g., Gal 3:7). Also, as you know, I hear the two Testaments telling a single Story of which we're a part. See Ben Witherington III, *Biblical Theology: The Convergence of the Canon* (New York: Cambridge University Press, 2019): "While it is certainly true that Paul sees the New Covenant as the fulfillment of the Abrahamic covenant and the replacement for the Mosaic covenant, he certainly does not see Christianity as replacing Judaism. Indeed, *for Paul, being in Christ, the Jewish messiah, is simply the proper development of the one people of God.* The people of God has become Jew and Gentile united in the Jewish messiah" (p. 342, emphasis mine).

[8] Most scholars seem to have a hard time identifying this "promise of the Spirit" in the Old Testament. See, for example, John R. Levison, *Filled with the Spirit* (Grand Rapids: Wm. B. Eerdmans Publishing, 2009), p. 270: "It is difficult to identify which promise Paul recalls here. The promise of outpouring upon sons and daughters, old and young, male and female slaves in Joel 3:1-4 (Eng. 2:28-32), which is cited in Acts 2:17-21, could be construed as a promise to the nations, though its context in Joel is centered upon Israel, and even Peter, in the Pentecost sermon in Acts, appears to interpret its fulfillment exclusively in relation to Israel (Acts 2:38-39). The reference may be more general. We have seen that Paul understands the spirit as the seal and pledge of God's promises (2 Cor 1:15-22), and the author of the letter to the Ephesians brings a lengthy opening prayer with a reference to 'the seal of the promised holy spirit; this is the pledge of our inheritance toward redemption as God's own people . . .' (Eph 1:13-14). He concludes a catena of Israelite scriptures that support his mission to the nations with the prayer, 'May the God of hope fill you with all joy and peace in believing, so that you may abound in hope by the power of the holy spirit' (Rom 15:13)." Yes, I think the reference has a "more general" sense, as we'll see; but I think it must also have at least one particular referent, so I think it's both. My reading presupposes that the New Testament authors weren't just interpreting and looking for *individual texts* of Scripture to help make sense of the work of God among

them. They actually *inhabited* the Story those texts are telling, and thus were able to discern connections and patters not immediately obvious when we're looking for evidence of this "promise" only in individual texts and events in the Old Testament. This hermeneutical presupposition is at the heart of Iain Provan's thesis regarding "the right reading of Scripture" (how the apostles read them), in *The Reformation and the Right Reading of Scripture* (Waco, TX: Baylor University Press, 2017)—the best treatment I've found so far on the nature of Scripture. An excellent example of such a reading of Scripture is that of Willem A. VanGemeren and Andrew Abernethy, "The Spirit and the Future: A Canonical Approach," in *Presence, Power and Promise: The Role of the Spirit of God in the Old Testament*, eds. David G. Firth and Paul D. Wegner (Downers Grove: IVP Academic, 2011). I will be drawing heavily on their work in what follows. See also Andrew K. Gabriel, "The Holy Spirit and Eschatology—with Implications for Ministry and the Doctrine of Spirit Baptism," *Journal of Pentecostal Theology* 25, no. 2 (September 10, 2016): pp. 203–21, https://doi.org/10.1163/17455251-02502004.

[9] David A. deSilva, *The Letter to the Galatians* (Grand Rapids: Wm. B. Eerdmans Publishing, 2018), p. 303: "On what basis could Paul make this identification [that 'the Holy Spirit *is* the content of the blessing of Abraham that was promised to the nations'], when the Holy Spirit is not mentioned in the promises given to Abraham in Genesis? First, Paul, along with other Christian leaders, witnessed the Spirit coming upon all who trusted in Jesus, whether Jews or Gentiles. It was as universal in scope as had been the promise to Abraham: 'in you all the nations will be blessed' (Gen 12:3; Gal 3:8). Second, the giving of the Spirit signified the believers' adoption by God as sons and daughters; the phenomenon of being filled with the Spirit led the early Christians, who thenceforth called upon God as 'Abba, Father' (Gal 4:6–7), to understand this experience as a spiritual begetting by God's own self, making them spiritual children of Abraham (Gal 3:26–29; 4:21–28), just as Isaac was the spiritual child of Abraham, having been born on the basis of God's promise rather than on the basis of what was possible for the flesh." Richard Hays offers a similar explanation in *Echoes of Scripture in the Letters of Paul* (New Haven: Yale University Press, 1989). For Hays, however, the gift of the Spirit seems to *replace* the promise of land and descendants, as opposed to simply *fulfill* the promise of descendants (as deSilva reads it): "this experienced Spirit must be the promised blessing of which Scripture speaks" (Hays, p. 110).

[10] VanGemeren and Abernethy, "The Spirit and the Future," p. 345: "The entire [Old Testament] canon elicits a variety of expectations regarding the work of God's *rûah* [Spirit]. The Torah, Prophets, and Writings all associate with one another to elicit anticipation and hope pertaining to God acting

by the *rûah.* The most prominent expectations pertain to the Spirit's role in carrying out God's creative-redemptive plans and in equipping prophets, kings, and people to restore God's order in society and to participate in and await the coming of the new creation."

[11] See further, my discussion "On Ruach Elohim:" https://www.wayfinders. quest/on-ruach-elohim.html. Here's another summary of the meanings of Ruach Elohim, by Jack Levison, *Inspired: Holy Spirit and the Mind of Faith* (Grand Rapids: Wm. B. Eerdmans Publishing, 2013), p. 187: "The first move God makes in the entire sweep of scripture, in fact, entails the stirring of the ruach: 'the earth was a formless void and darkness covered the face of the deep, while a ruach of God swept over the face of the waters' (Gen. 1:2). Translations are not much help in figuring out what exactly this ruach is. One reads, 'a wind from God swept over the face of the water' (NRSV), another, 'God's wind swept over the waters' (CEB), and still others, 'the Spirit of God was hovering over the waters' (NIV) or 'God's Spirit brooded like a bird above the watery abyss' (The Message). The Hebrew word ruach does mean wind—'a wind from God swept over the face of the waters.' The water's untamed waves are stirred by wind, God's wind, so something good, something beautiful, must be yet to come. But the Hebrew word also means breath that produces words, as in the opening poem of the Bible, where God's powerful words divide darkness from light, sea from land, day from night (Gen. 1:1–2:4). The refrain 'And God said' gives structure and stability to creation, as life-ordering words are formed by spirit-breath rolling over God's tongue. Yet even wind and breath do not exhaust the mystery of God's spirit. The verb hover or sweep, which offers the first glimpse of the spirit's power in the Bible, occurs only once elsewhere in the Old Testament, when God is an eagle that 'stirs up its nest, and hovers over its young; as it spreads its wings, takes them up, and bears them aloft on its pinions' (Deut. 32:11-12). This is tender care, powerful pinions grasping Israel's neck to 'set it atop the heights of the land' (32:13). The spirit of God, at the birth of creation, hovers over an expectant earth, broods like a bird over the watery abyss—an eagle-like spirit poised with powerful wings over a fledgling creation. Order is on the horizon. Chaos is about to slip into nothingness."

[12] VanGemeren and Abernethy, "The Spirit and the Future," p. 327.

[13] Ibid., p. 331.

[14] Ibid., p. 330.

[15] As Christopher Wright points out, the coming of the Spirit was expected to bring restoration at all levels: "the *created order* (Is 32:15) will be renewed and restored to its full fertility and growth... the *moral order* (Is 32:16) will

be set right once again... the *social order* (Is 32:17–18) will be restored to *shalom.*" Christopher J. H. Wright, *Knowing the Holy Spirit Through the Old Testament* (Downers Grove: IVP Academic, 2006), pp. 123–125.

[16] On church history being part of the biblical Story, see ch. 1, under subsection "The Possibilities" (under section "A Biblical Metaphysics").

[17] David A. deSilva, *Transformation: The Heart of Paul's Gospel* (Bellingham: Lexham Press, 2014). See also Darrell L. Bock, *Recovering the Real Lost Gospel: Reclaiming the Gospel as Good News* (Nashville: B&H Academic, 2010). Here's the message that Bock finds at the center of the gospel: "God has taken the initiative in Jesus Christ to bring us into relationship with [Himself]. At the core of that good news stands a promise to form a new relationship and a new community. God was remaking a people He had previously formed around His law. That law had not led God's people into righteousness, not because the law was flawed, but because we were. For a relationship with God to function, a new work had to be done from within the depths of the human soul. So God offered the hope of a promise, the hope of His Spirit poured out in the last days, and the hope of a new responsiveness etched in His children's hearts" (p. 20).

[18] I'll expand on the Spirit's enabling in the rest of this chapter. For an exploration of how the Lord Jesus set us free on the cross, see ch. 3.

[19] "Indeed, [in Galatians] Paul advances a generative account of the Spirit as the Abrahamic blessing that grasps us through the gospel of the Crucified and so gives rise to forms of life consistent with the new creation." Christopher R. J. Holmes, "The Spirit and the Promise: On Becoming Aligned with the Way Things Really Are," in *Apocalyptic and the Future of Theology: With and Beyond J. Louis Martyn,* eds. Joshua B. Davis and Douglas Harink (Eugene, OR: Cascade Books, 2012), p. 220. I haven't heard very good things from my top sources about the work of J. Louis Martyn on eschatology, but this statement by Holmes—in a collection of essays that take their "point of departure from the work of Martyn"—seems to me right on.

[20] On this, see Gordon D. Fee, *Paul, the Spirit, and the People of God* (Grand Rapids: Baker Academic, 1996), p. 14.

[21] N. T. Wright and Michael F. Bird, *The New Testament in Its World: An Introduction to the History, Literature, and Theology of the First Christians* (Grand Rapids: Zondervan Academic, 2019), p. 377: "The christology of 'divine identity' is thus matched by the pneumatology of 'divine identity,' in both cases focused in particular on the Jewish eschatology of the return of YHWH."

[22] "The coming and presence of the Spirit is simultaneous with the coming and presence of Christ." Holmes, "The Spirit and the Promise," p. 221.

[23] Gordon Fee, *Paul, the Spirit and the People of God,* pp. 25–26.

[24] Fee, id.

[25] F. F. Bruce, *The Gospel of John: Introduction, Exposition, Notes,* 3rd ed. (Grand Rapids: Wm. B. Eerdmans Publishing, 1994), pp. 303–304 (emphasis added).

[26] It's worth quoting Margaret S. Archer, Andrew Collier, and Douglas V. Porpora here again (as in ch. 2, n. 7), in their "What Do We Mean by God?" in *Transcendence: Critical Realism and God* (New York: Routledge, 2004), p. 39: "The work of God in this world—a work that involves human agents—is in the first place a work of undoing this alienation [between God and his creatures] by making God's presence manifest in all things. But we can go further and say that it is the purpose of God, without abolishing the distinction between God and creatures, to take up these creatures into God's own self so that they can participate in the divine nature and God can be all in all. To join in this work is the highest goal of humankind. It involves in the first place our own union with God; but it also involves the redemption of creation."

[27] I am indebted to J. Richard Middleton for this insight on the "plot structure" of the biblical story. See Middleton, *A New Heaven and a New Earth: Reclaiming Biblical Eschatology* (Grand Rapids: Baker Academic, 2014), ch. 3, "The Plot of the Biblical Story."

[28] Let me add here that talk about oneness with God is not to confuse our identity with God's, since "agency per se carries no ontological implications." Philip Alexander, "'The Agent of the King Is Treated as the King Himself': Does the Worship of Jesus Imply His Divinity?" in *In the Fullness of Time: Essays on Christology, Creation, and Eschatology in Honor of Richard Bauckham,* eds. Daniel M. Gurtner, Grant Macaskill, and Jonathan T. Pennington (Grand Rapids: Wm. B. Eerdmans Publishing, 2016), p. 113: "Not enough attention has been paid to the concept of agency. An agent can be offered the same respect as the principal whom he represents (as in the case of the king as God's representative on earth), but the agent and the principal who sent him may belong to different orders of being (as, again, in the case of the king and God). If Christ is the agent, indeed the supreme agent, of God's purposes in the world, then that carries in itself no implication as to his nature, and certainly does not imply that he belongs to the same order of being as God, still less that he is God. Agency per se carries no ontological implications." The Lord Jesus' own ontological oneness with the

Father, however, does seem evident nonetheless: "Who, being *in very nature* God, did not consider equality with God something to be used to his own advantage" (Phil 2:6). See also n. 43 of this chapter.

[29] Notice also that this "breath of life" given to us in Genesis 2:7 is called our "spirit" in Psalm 146:3–4: "When their spirit *[rûaḥ]* departs, they return to the ground." Jack Levison (same person as John Levison, quoted previously) explains that "with this description of death, the psalmist has replaced the original breath of life (nišmaṯ ḥayyîm) of Genesis 2:7 with spirit (rûaḥ), although the meaning seems to be much the same." Levison, *Boundless God* (Grand Rapids: Baker Academic, 2020), p. 27. Not only that, but "this understanding of rûaḥ in the Jewish Scriptures mirrors a point Pannenberg makes from a Christian perspective: 'In an extended sense the breath of life that is already given to all of us at creation (Gen. 2:7) may be seen as endowment with God's Spirit'" (ibid., p. 169), quoting Wolfhart Pannenberg, *Systematic Theology,* trans. Geoffrey W. Bromiley (Grand Rapids: Wm. B. Eerdmans Publishing, 1997), p. 9.

[30] Middleton, *A New Heaven and a New Earth*, p. 48.

[31] Id.

[32] Ibid., p. 49.

[33] See ch. 2 for more on this.

[34] See Raymond C. Van Leeuwen, "Cosmos, Temple, House: Building and Wisdom in Ancient Mesopotamia and Israel," in *From the Foundations to the Crenellations: Essays on Temple Building in the Ancient Near East and Hebrew Bible*, eds. Mark J. Boda and Jamie Novotny, Alter Orient Und Altes Testament 366 (Münster: Ugarit-Verlag, 2010), pp. 399–421; and Rikk E. Watts, "The New Exodus/New Creational Restoration of the Image of God," in *What Does It Mean to Be Saved? Broadening Evangelical Horizons of Salvation*, ed. John G. Stackhouse Jr. (Grand Rapids: Baker Academic, 2002), esp. pp. 18–23.

[35] Middleton, *A New Heaven and a New Earth*: "Genesis 1 ultimately envisions the development of all aspects of culture, technology, and civilization. Humans are to accomplish this development as God's representatives, which is the upshot of being made in the 'image' and 'likeness' of God ... an echo can be heard here of the Psalm 8:5 reference to humans made 'a little lower than God'" (p. 43).

[36] For a fuller explanation of the image and likeness of God as referring primarily to *offspring* (or "sonship"), including Scripture references and other reliable secondary sources, see ch. 2, n. 8.

[37] The picture here, to the best of my understanding, is that of humans who might not even know about the God of Israel—and who certainly don't have what had been revealed to Israel, but who nonetheless have come to know about realities one would not expect them to know about, unless God had also revealed it to them some other way. Now, they're certainly confused about what or who can be rightly called "the image of God," but they obviously know a lot about how God works through image-bearing. How these peoples were able to discern such metaphysical realities is a subject for another day, but it might have something to do with what Paul has in mind in Romans 1:18–32, where he says that "what may be known about God is plain to them, because God has made it plain to them" (v. 19). However, if we take seriously the intertestamental developments regarding what's going on in the *spirit-realm,* much of which is legitimated in the New Testament, perhaps we would understand some of these insights as revealed to the nations by spirits, via their own priests. Michael Heiser might have something to say on this, given his work on *The Unseen Realm: Recovering the Supernatural Worldview of the Bible* (Bellingham: Lexham Press, 2019), and on *Demons: What the Bible Really Says About the Powers of Darkness* (Bellingham: Lexham Press, 2020). In any case, they were able to discern, for example, that humans are children of God (Acts 17:28), and Paul simply agrees, legitimating their insight, just as the author of Genesis 2 legitimates something of the ancient Mesopotamian understanding of the image of a god and how it supposedly comes alive. It is not the idols of the nations that represent the true God, says Genesis 2, but *we* human beings—all of us—we are "the decisive locus of divine presence on earth" (Middleton).

[38] Middleton, *A New Heaven and a New Earth,* p. 49.

[39] Rikk E. Watts, "The New Exodus/New Creational Restoration of the Image of God," p. 22 (emphasis mine).

[40] Id.

[41] Craig S. Keener, *The Gospel of John: Two Volumes* (Grand Rapids: Baker Academic, 2010), under sub-section "Empowerment for the Mission (20:22)," Scribd e-book.

[42] In terms of the *content* of our calling as children of God, I'm keeping it very general here given the nature of my current inquiry, but there's obviously a lot we could say. Most important, I think, is our posture and the sorts of people

God expects us to be if we're going to reflect who *he* is, and thus represent him well. Here's an excellent summary of what he himself would say: "He has shown you, O mortal, what is good. And what does the LORD require of you? *To act justly and to love mercy and to walk humbly with your God"* (Mic 6:8). "The good news," explains deSilva, "is that God lavishly supplies all that is needed for us to walk in righteousness and enjoy the consequences of living righteous lives. What is required of us is, essentially, to cultivate awareness (including honesty with ourselves before God and one another) and steady commitment as we consistently invest ourselves and our resources as the Spirit directs and empowers" (*The Letter to the Galatians,* p. 499). For a glimpse of the picture I see as regards our calling, in light of God's intentions for the work of his hands, see my reflections on "What Matters Most:" https://www.wayfinders.quest/what-matters-most.html.

[43] Here's Brenda B. Colijn again (see also ch. 2, n. 7), in her *Images of Salvation in the New Testament* (Downers Grove: IVP Academic, 2010): "Eternal life is the eschatological gift of God, the life of the kingdom of God in the age to come. It is everlasting life. More importantly, it has the qualities of joy and completeness that characterize the life of God. In fact, it *is* the life of God mediated to human beings by the Son of God and generated in them by the Spirit of God.... Those who come to know Jesus begin to experience a life that is shaped and sustained by the love of God in Christ. This life cannot be touched by death, and it will be perfected in the resurrection" (p. 99). Again, that's because "the infusion of the Spirit into the life of the believers brings Christ's life into theirs..." (deSilva, *Galatians*, p. 470). From the perspective of a more systematic theology, see Andrew Wright, *Christianity and Critical Realism: Ambiguity, Truth and Theological Literacy* (New York: Routledge, 2012), pp. 175–76: "A number of New Testament passages refer to the future participation of humanity in the being of God: the gifts conferred upon the world by Jesus Christ are given 'so that through them you might escape from the corruption that is in the world because of lust, and may become *participants in the divine nature'* (2 Peter 1:4; emphasis added). ... Just as the persons of the Trinity are united in perfect reciprocal love, and just as the human and divine natures of the incarnate Son were similarly united in hypostatic union, so human beings will enter into just such a relationship with their Creator. This does not imply the dissolution of human identity within the Godhead: just as the bond of love that unites the Trinity simultaneously upholds the unique identities of the three persons, so the perfect bond of love between the Creator and his creatures will uphold the individual identities of both God and individual human beings. With the perfection of creation, God's perfect love of humanity will finally be reciprocated by humankind's perfect love of God. The ontological achievement of the hypostatic union

between the human and divine natures of Christ prefigures the participation of humanity in the divine nature, and the perfection of their status as creatures created in the image of God."

[44] Hopkins, "God's Grandeur," in *The New Oxford Book of English Verse,* ed. H. Gardner (New York: Oxford University Press, 1972), p. 786.

PART III
Getting Our Story Straight

Do not conform to the pattern [the stories] of this world, but be transformed by the renewing of your mind. Then you will be able to test and approve what God's will is—his good, pleasing and perfect will.
(Rom 12:2)

To be converted to Christ is to be turned from the world as one has known it and to see everything anew in the context of Christ. It is to be radically reoriented; it is to find new bearings from Christ. In this new orientation, the gospel of Jesus Christ engages us to our personal depths, permeating our imaginative world in a quite comprehensive way. Jesus Christ—in words and actions culminating in his embrace of execution and his resurrection—reveals and embodies the approach of God in sovereignty as our ultimate context. In Christ, God engages our familiar contexts comprised of our habitual practices and assumptions, worldviews, and personal commitments, and breaks them open, animating them as signs pointing to the deeper context of his approaching kingdom and liberating us for participation in it. —David J. Kettle[1]

---

[1] David J. Kettle, *Western Culture in Gospel Context: Towards the Conversion of the West* (Eugene, OR: Cascade Books, 2011), pp. 2–3.

CHAPTER 5
The Body of Christ in a World of Competing Narratives

We live in a world of competing narratives. In the end, we have to decide for ourselves which is right. And having made that decision, we then need to inhabit the story we trust. —Alister E. McGrath[1]

Introduction

It's actually understandable and natural to take for granted the narratives into which we're born and raised. And it would be ideal if we didn't have to question those narratives. A healthy and strong sense of self depends on our confidence in them. We need that. So, although I am here precisely to question and sort out narratives, this is not as an end in itself. I just want to be at home in God's world, and I see no other way.

Tracking with God

I think as Christians we *should* take for granted the narratives we have received from our Christian forebears and traditions. This should be our initial and default posture.[2] How else will we receive and pass on the apostolic tradition? How else will we sustain a strong sense of identity as the people of God?

But because of our fickleness, because of our tendency to go astray, and because *there are* competing narratives (even within the church), each generation should also find ways to ask ourselves: Are we still doing the "Abraham, Isaac and Jacob" thing: is their Story our story? Are we still echoing the gospel that Jesus preached? Do we know what it means? Are we tracking with God and what he's up to? Are we marching to his beat?

Contested Territory

The church lives to embody a reality, and to pass on a message, against which there is fierce opposition. The very narrative we're called to inhabit witnesses to this. The Lord is making all things new, yes, but not everyone is onboard. We can expect competing agendas behind competing narratives.

> We must beware—not categorically avoid, but beware—any alliance with the powers: powers of government, powers of commerce, powers of ideology, powers of entertainment. Such alliances always will tend to draw us away from the Lordship of Christ and toward idolatry. Ultimately, we cannot serve two masters, and we must be vigilant against any alluring inclination to think we can. We can cooperate with the powers as far as such cooperation produces *shalom* and avoids worse evil. But we must also simply expect "tribulation" in the world (Jn. 16:33) from those powers, since our loyalties are elsewhere and higher, and conflict is inevitable. —John Stackhouse, *Making the Best of It: Following Christ in the Real World* [3]

That is, of course, *if* our highest allegiance is indeed with God. But if we are indeed with God, if we're *his* agents in the world, then we can't afford to get our Story confused and lose sight of what's really going on. According to the Scriptures, *the world* can't afford it.[4]

It's tricky though, isn't it? Tricky and hard to sort out, never mind live it out. And it would be much easier if we could stay in our own subcultures to avoid confusion, but that's not what the Lord said to do. We're called to remain in the world God is trying to redeem—present and engaged with the rest of humanity (Matt 28:16–20; Mark 12:30–31; John 17:13–19).

Of course, we're culture makers too and do have subcultures. Who else will make culture that is pleasing to God if not the people of God? It's just that he's drawing the whole world to himself, so we need to keep our culture-making public and open to the public (2 Cor 5:19–20). In fact, if God is who he says he is, and if the gospel = reality, then there's nothing more promising on the face of the earth than children of God being children of God—filling the world with his life and his light.

But before we can shed much light in the world, we need to let it shine on ourselves, don't we? Let's take a look at ourselves then, before the Lord, and see what we find.

Cultural Confusion

As culture makers by design, the Lord gives us freedom to build on his creation—even at the level of meaning (Gen 1:26–28; 2:19–20).[5] As we discussed in Chapter 1, much of reality as we experience it is a social construction: a dense web of meaning that *we* have created through the ages, beginning with our use of language. This is actually good and how the Lord intends it, but we need to be mindful of it.

We need to keep in mind that the cultural waters in which we swim—the worlds of meaning in which we've been brought up—are not the only option. And this applies to Christian worlds of meaning too. They *could* be otherwise and still be "biblical" and pleasing to God. It is of the nature of things that we can live out the life of God in endless ways, potentially looking nothing like our last couple thousand years. Just saying, let's not straitjacket the gospel with our frameworks and mental models.

Even our identities, individual and collective, are not bound to past and present realities alone. Yes, we need to look back to know where we come from, but the Story keeps going and it's taking us with it: we are who we are *becoming.* And that's in the hands of the One "making all things new" (Rev 21:5 CEB; cf. 2 Cor 5:17). In that sense, we come from the future.[6]

Going Astray

If I'm reading church history right, we also need ways to routinely test our worlds of meaning in the light of Scripture—at least one intentional review or revision per generation (Vatican II–style, if we have to). We *can* get it wrong, can't we?

> The mantra of the American Dream is to advance yourself: "with hard work, ingenuity, innovation, you can have it all!"
>
> The frightening reality of the gospel: Jesus *does* call us to give up everything we have. And he may tell any one of us to sell all of our possessions and give them to the poor. But we don't believe this!
>
> If we form Jesus to look like us and be who we want him to be, then even when we gather together and sing our praises and lift our hands, the reality is we are not worshiping the Jesus of the Bible. We are worshipping and singing to ourselves. —David Platt[7]

I think Platt hit the nail on the head with this diagnosis. And I'm a witness. I once heard and came to embrace a gospel that was indistinguishable from the American Dream. Now, my issue is not with the American Dream per se—or any other dream. That's not my business. What disturbs me is how we have confused the gospel with it.

What *is* the American Dream anyway? It depends on who's dreaming it, doesn't it?[8] Well, God too has a dream, and he's been telling us all about it since Genesis 1.

God's Dream

It turns out that God's dream has a great deal in common with our national and personal dreams. And that's because he made us *for life,* which is precisely what we're after, however broken and misguided our ways of seeking it might be.[9] The greatest difference I see between his dream and ours is that his is *big,* and ours is ridiculously puny. Even our usual "God loves you and has a wonderful plan for your life" pales in comparison with what he actually said: "See, I am making *all things* new" (Rev 21:5 CEB).[10]

And so we go in our little worlds, anxiously seeking our own well-being—prosperity, "success," whatever you want to call it—badly confused, thinking that life is all *about me.* And we end up wasting our lives seeking life in all the wrong places (Matt 6:25–34).[11]

Do we not know that the meaning and purpose of life is actually found in God's own vision for the work of his hands? Are we tracking with *that?* Because, in a sense, that vision *is* the gospel. His invitation is to come out of our little worlds (out of ourselves) and into the cosmic Story he's set in motion—a Story in which, according to the Scriptures, we have a crucial role to play (Gen 1:26–28; Matt 28:18–20). But if the Lord Jesus is to be our model, that role is decidedly *not* to look after ourselves (Phil 2:1–8; 1 Pet 2:21).

> *The church is the church only when it exists for others.*
> —Dietrich Bonhoeffer[12]

Humans are made in the image and likeness of One who is Love (Gen 1:26–28; 1 John 4:7–21; 1 Cor 12:31b–13:13).[13] And, as such, we're made *to care*—to be *for* the other—which is the true meaning of "love."[14]

God made us to care for this wonderful planet and all who live in it, including ourselves, but not just ourselves (Gen 1:26–28; Lev

19:18; Mark 12:31). And so, for instance, we can't just live in a culture that runs on competition without feeling uneasy about it (at least at some level), precisely because we're *for* those against whom we're supposed to be competing! But we do. And instead of redeeming and blessing our cultures by sharing the culture of heaven on earth, we go on living for ourselves just like everybody else.[15] Why is that? Because by assimilating aspects of our surrounding culture *uncritically,* and for whatever reason, we end up inhabiting the stories in which those ways of being make sense. And the result, for one thing, is *the weakening of our confidence* as characters in the Story the Bible itself is telling.

Our confidence is weak because we know in our guts that something's off at the level of *meaning.* And of course something's off, if the stories we're actually enacting don't square with the one we claim is true! I believe there lies the greatest source of all the half-heartedness, the depressing numbness, we see in the church today. We've got to sort this out.[16]

Other Voices
This is pretty much what James K. A. Smith has pointed out in *Desiring the Kingdom,* about the idolatries of *consumerism, nationalism,* and the "sacrificial violence" of the "military-entertainment complex."[17] N. T. Wright has said something similar in regard to *neo-Gnosticism, "the new imperialism,"* and the meaningless extremes of *postmodernism (Creation, Power and Truth: The Gospel in a World of Cultural Confusion).*[18]

Walter Brueggemann put it this way:

> The contemporary American church is so largely enculturated to the American ethos of consumerism that it has little power to believe or to act. This enculturation is in some way true across the spectrum of church life, both liberal and conservative. It may not be a new

situation, but it is one that seems especially urgent and pressing at the present time. That enculturation is true not only of the institution of the church but also of us as persons. Our consciousness has been claimed by false fields of perception and idolatrous systems of language and rhetoric. —Brueggemann, *The Prophetic Imagination*[19]

Let's hear a few other voices, to get a better sense of the nature of these "false fields of perception and idolatrous systems of language and rhetoric."

Religion is important to Americans. But the religion we practice is often not the religion we confess. From at least the time of Alexis de Tocqueville, observers of the American scene have recognized the essence of religion in everything American. Let's be honest with ourselves. Even though some Americans claim the country's population is deeply divided, often described as engaged in a "culture war," most Americans tend to worship at similar altars. Americans form a nation of believers; but what do they believe? What is the object of their faithful devotion?

Americans believe, first, in a serviceable God. We want a God who meets our needs, who provides altars where we can get good service. Second, we want a friendly God, who blesses us as we become comfortable, wealthy, and successful. Our altars provide places where we find blessing in a community of like-minded seekers. Americans are practical people, who want a pragmatic faith. The objects of our attention have become our God, and fulfilling our desires has become our religion. —Juan M. Floyd-Thomas, et al., *The Altars Where We Worship)*[20]

By "the altars where we worship" they mean *body and sex, big business, entertainment, politics, sports, science and technology.*

They observe that we "attest to being religious and/or spiritual in conventional ways while, at the same time, in actual practice, [we] find meaning in altars found in popular culture." Indeed, we're "able to find gratification and sustenance at these altars, and are able to offer adoration and reverence before them, all without experiencing even the slightest twinge of cognitive dissonance or pang of disloyalty where traditional religious associations are concerned."[21]

Sounds like the message of Hosea all over again. And just like Gomer—the prostitute Hosea had to marry in order to sympathize and speak for God—it wasn't for lack of resources that we've gone astray, or was it? Lack of guidance? Lack of nerve?

> *You do not have, because you do not ask. You ask and do not receive, because you ask wrongly, in order to spend what you get on your pleasures. Adulterers! Do you not know that friendship with the world is enmity with God? ... Or do you suppose that it is for nothing that the scripture says, "God yearns jealously for the spirit that he has made to dwell in us"?* (Jas 4:2b–4a, 5 NRSV)

James doesn't mince words. Only we need a nuanced understanding of what "friendship with the world" means here. Those who love their neighbors are surely their friends. I'm sure he wouldn't have us shun the world if we're meant to be salt and light in it (Matt 5:13–16).

So, how do we navigate life in this tension? How do we remain at home in our own Story, and remain loyal to our Maker, while enjoying meaningful relationships with others who live in other worlds and worship other gods?

> Scripture and Tradition provide the church with a distinctive kind of existence—with unique ways of birthing and dying, of becoming youthful and growing old, of marrying and remaining single, of celebrating and sacrificing, of thinking and imagining, of worshipping the true God and protesting against false gods. ... these distinctive beliefs and practices constitute the church's own culture. —Ralph Wood, *Contending for the Faith*[22]

Scripture and tradition provide us with "a distinctive kind of existence" but what that existence will look like in any given generation, that is not given us. That is *our* task to discern and live out as we play our part faithfully in each generation. That's part of the beauty, and the dangers, of the freedom the Lord has given us as children of God. All he seems to ask is that we live and build in line with his own character, according to what he has revealed about his vision for the work of his hands.

> Of course, we know *that* we are to maintain faithful, committed relationships, even in the midst of a culture of convenience. We know *that* we are to practice justice, and economic stewardship, even in a society of power grabs and unlimited consumption. The trouble is that *how* we are to embody these admirable goals is not specified. The Bible is neither strictly a script for us to enact nor a rule book or repository of timeless truths into which we can dip when we need guidance. ... This does not mean that we have no guidance for our improvisation. Apart from the canonical givenness of Scripture as the authoritative story in terms of which we are to read our lives, we have access to the Author of the story [through his Spirit]. —Richard Middleton and Brian Walsh, *Truth Is Stranger Than It Used to Be: Biblical Faith in a Postmodern Age*[23]

The question for us, though, is where to go from here. Our surrounding culture has sucked us in to the point that the world has a hard time distinguishing those who know God from those who don't. Not necessarily an issue, perhaps, but given the evidence above we do have an issue. And the task is as daunting as it is exhilarating. Daunting for obvious reasons. Exhilarating because who knows what the Lord has up his sleeve this time. We have the same Spirit that raised the Lord Jesus from the dead, and then turned the world upside down in the first century (Luke 24; Acts 17:6). If only we come home to our own Story, and learn to keep in step with the Spirit (Gal 5:25), he surely would surprise the world again.[24]

Popular Culture
And what about popular culture, what do we make of it?

> Popular culture affects us and those around us on the level of worldview—the assumptions we make about reality every day—often without our realizing it. This worldview effect is both obvious and elusive: we know it happens, but we don't often stop to think about what it means. How should we respond when our worldview is challenged? Though it might be tempting to move to a high and lofty mountain to avoid popular culture altogether, such a tactic usually doesn't work; you only end up creating another type of popular culture. Rather, I believe that a Christian's proper response to a worldview challenge from popular culture is to ask questions, to understand from a biblical perspective what popular culture is and how it works. —Ted Turnau, *Popologetics: Popular Culture in Christian Perspective*[25]

I agree. I actually see much that is good, fun (in a good way), and very meaningful in popular culture—though it certainly is a mixed bag, and we do need to be careful. But regardless of what we find in our surrounding culture, I think we need to remain engaged with others in the world, even though we live in very different worlds of meaning. My approach would be something close to that of Paul M. Gould and Ted Turnau: trying to understand the culture from within our own Story, so we can be helpful witnesses across worldviews in meaningful relationships with our neighbors.[26] But let's not get our Story confused; that's not good for anyone.

> A biblical worldview helps us to sort out the good from the bad. Our task as Christians, then, is to respond to popular culture as a messy, deeply meaningful mixture. And I believe the only appropriate response to something that messy and that meaningful is apologetics. —Ted Turnau[27]

I think it's going to take more than apologetics, but that's certainly an important part of the picture. I'll leave it at that for the moment, but I can already see that my approach will be to focus first on the existential questions these realities raise *for us,* as God's people, and then live the implications *from the inside out,* so that our apologetics can be a genuine and caring expression of the hope and the light that is in us.

Eschatological Confusion
So what is the Christian hope, then? I've always found this so essential to the life of faith. So much hangs on whether the plan is to restore the earth, or to destroy it and move on to another form of existence.

In my experience, there's a lot of confusion in the church on this question. I had to do a lot of digging to finally get clarity on this. To see that God's plan is to restore this world we live in. That heaven is coming here, and that we're going nowhere (Rev 3:12; 5:10; 21:2). That this is home.[28]

But the confusion is nothing new. It seems that as far back as the second century the church was already losing its grip on the nature of the Christian hope.[29] I find this astonishing. To think that we started losing sight of God's vision for the work of his hands so soon after the apostles. A vision that, in biblical faith, has always been of holistic and cosmic *renewal,* not some disembodied existence in heaven, as so many still maintain.

Thankfully, the church has been recovering the biblical vision increasingly, especially since the twentieth century.

> When an organization associated with Billy Graham (who has historically sounded like D. L. Moody, with his lifeboat theology), produces a document that affirms the redemption of this world, it is clear that we are in the midst of a paradigm shift. —Richard Middleton, *A New Heaven and a New Earth* (referring to the Lausanne Committee for World Evangelization)[30]

Contemplative Confusion
I also have questions about the metaphysical presuppositions in much of the literature on *contemplative prayer.*[31]

I've always been intrigued by contemplative prayer. So much about it makes sense to me, as you can see it already in my online discussion on "Our Sense of Self."[32] There, I recommend *mindfulness* meditation to my readers because I wrote that discussion with a secular audience in mind, and mindfulness has been secularized for therapeutic purposes. I've found mindfulness a very helpful starting point from which to develop my own contemplative practice (organically) before the Lord.

The main limitation of mindfulness is that it focuses only on "the present moment," which is very effective for psychological and neurophysiological healing, but it's limited as a "spiritual" practice for Christians inhabiting the biblical Story of reality.[33]

We need meditation practices that promote what Daniel Siegel calls "narrative integration" (of past, present, and future), helping us be at home in the story of our lives, and—I would add—in the Story of reality.[34] Biblical contemplation, it seems to me, is contemplation *within* the biblical Story, and about what's going on in that Story: God, his ways, his world, our place in that world, and so forth.

My top source on mindfulness, Prof. Mark Williams (Oxford), is actually Christian—an ordained minister in the Anglican communion. He's the founding director of the Oxford Mindfulness Centre, and he's done a great job removing religious and metaphysical baggage from the content of mindfulness teaching in his work.[35]

When it comes to the contemplative prayer literature, however, I have a hard time entrusting myself to the guides available. And that's a shame because I want to develop my contemplative practice in conversation with the Christian tradition. I just can't relate to the worlds of meaning invoked in the literature. They seem to have moved too far from the biblical Story I'm trying to inhabit.

Two issues come to mind (though they're probably related): a *static* view of things and a heavy dose of Platonism or dualism.

A Higher Realm

It feels as though they're trying to rise above the physical in their spirituality, while I personally don't even like to separate the two. I see the spiritual and the physical as inseparable dimensions of *one reality*.[36] Biblical spirituality, it seems to me, is an embodied and earthy engagement with God and his world, a world that is both spiritual and physical, and which he pronounced intrinsically good as a whole (Gen 1).

As embodied creatures by design, it is precisely as *physical* creatures that we should be praying and relating to God. I want to get to know the Lord in acts of contemplation, but I envision earthy, embodied, acts of contemplation. And in my experience, the contemplative prayer literature falls short of this.

Mindfulness meditation, on the other hand, feels more natural, organic, earthy. I feel more human when I practice, more present, without having to escape my physicality. (It depends on who guides you, though—much of the literature on mindfulness also carries metaphysical baggage that doesn't square with biblical metaphysics.)

A Strange World

The world of meaning I encounter in the contemplative prayer literature is also quite static, not dynamic and relational, as the biblical world of meaning and as I normally experience reality. Perhaps this is just another angle on things, part of the Greek contribution to good culture-making. Please explain this to me if this is the case. But it seems to me that if we can't recognize the biblical world of meaning from within our constructions of reality, as Christians— the stewards of the gospel, we have a problem.

So let's make sure we have this conversation. There's too much at stake to be passive on these questions, and risk living our lives with a warped understanding of reality.[37]

A Spirituality of the Senses

One exception I found to this pattern within the Christian tradition is the Ignatian Examen.[38] The Daily Examen offers similar psychological benefits to those of mindfulness, in my experience, and it focuses on the Presence of God and where we stand before him, which brings us pretty close to a "biblical" contemplative practice.

Etcetera, etcetera, etcetera…

Much more could be said regarding narrative confusion in the Body of Christ. I offer these reflections as a witness who's had to wrestle particularly with the issues and questions I engaged above, but clearly there's more.[39]

See also my discussion on the doctrine of *felix culpa* (Addendum 1), my stance on the "Athens versus Jerusalem" debate (in Chapter 1),[40] and my "Competing Narratives: A Reflection" (Addendum 2)—a Scripture reflection that became a telling of the gospel in a prophetic voice.

Addendum 1

A Happy Fall?

I first ran into the doctrine of *felix culpa* (or "happy fall") while listening to a beautiful song by Audrey Assad, "Fortunate Fall."[41] I had been listening to the whole album and was loving it, even this song, until I realized what it was saying—and I was shocked. "Fortunate fall?!"

I ran into it again during a seminary course I was taking online, when a classmate asked me what I thought about the doctrine. I had been expressing my views about the need to inhabit the biblical Story, and he thought it would be interesting to know what I thought about this particular doctrine. He explained:

> Theologians like Augustine, Aquinas, and Liebniz all utilize it in their explanations for the existence of evil and the fall. They say something like "God saw it as better to bring good out of evil than to not let any evil exist at all." So the Felix Culpa as used by Leibniz argues that this is the best of all possible worlds because things like redemption are possible which would not be possible if there had been no fall. Maybe you could say, this is the "best of all possible stories" given that the fall is a reality and God will overcome it to redeem us.[42]

I looked into it a bit to answer his question, and I explained that I don't agree with Leibniz that this is the best of all possible worlds. If you ask me, the best of all possible worlds is one in which God's will is done "as it is in heaven" (Matt 6:10).

I think I can say with confidence that "the fall" of Genesis 3 was not the will of God. I know because he prohibited the actions that led to it (Gen 2:15–17), and then even regretted having created us, seeing the bloody mess that followed (6:6). Obviously, when someone committed a grievous sin in Israel, there was no hint that something promising had happened. No, "stone them" is what the Torah said to do: "You must purge the evil from among you" (e.g., Deut 17:7; cf. 17:12; 19:13, 19, etc.).

I don't see how "redemption" could be the best possible scenario either. The need for redemption implies that something has gone wrong and needs to be addressed. Yet, in Genesis 1—where we see God bring about his desires for creation without opposition—everything was "good" and "very good" without anything needing redemption. Isn't the will of a wise and loving creator precisely what defines what is good for his creation? If creation was "very good" in God's estimation, still in the absence of anything needing redemption, then what makes us think that the need for redemption was somehow a good thing?

The Lord Jesus clearly didn't want the cup he had to drink to bring about our redemption (Matt 26:39). Yet somehow we have come up with a doctrine that teaches it *was* a good thing he had to drink it.

Now, I think it's obvious that God brings good out of evil. He does it again and again: from Joseph's slavery in Egypt, to Israel's stumbling (Rom 11:11–12), to the cross. But that cannot mean that it was good that evil happened in the first place.

It means, first of all, that God is so committed to us and so wise and so powerful that he can take us through *despite* what happened. The fact that he uses the evil itself to bring something good is secondary: *the sort of thing he does with what he's working with.* This cannot mean, however, that the fall of Genesis 3 was a happy fall—at least not according to the biblical story itself. Not if our wise and loving Father said not to do it. He said not to do it because it *wasn't* a good thing to do.

When it comes to the question of evil, it helps me to remember that God doesn't tell us everything. And knowing us, I wouldn't either if I were him, lest we ruin everything (1 Cor 2:7–8)! So, as we try to make sense of such difficult questions as these (why he allowed evil in creation at all, etc.), we need to keep in mind that we probably don't have all the data.

One piece of the puzzle we do have, one that is often missing in our sensemaking, is the *spiritual dimension* of reality. We tend to build our worldviews and theological frameworks without taking into account the reality, presence, and roles of spirit-beings in the biblical Story. The answer to Daniel's prayer, for instance, was delayed by some spirit-being preventing God's messenger from reaching Daniel (Dan 10:1–14). We don't know what might have been going on all along in the spirit-realm that might shed light on our questions about evil and God's ways. We need to leave room in the picture for that.[43]

I took a quick look at what my sources might say about the doctrine of *felix culpa,* and they seem to feel about the same as I do.[44]

Actually, N. T. Wright seems willing to grant a sort of *felix culpa* in God's use of Israel's stumbling (their unfaithfulness to the covenant), for the sake of the inclusion of the nations.

> If there is a felix culpa theology in the New Testament, it is perhaps at this point. Not the sin of Adam, about which there was nothing felix, not even in the long prospect of 'such a great redeemer.' If I have under-stood Paul, he would have said that the one who was from all eternity 'equal with God,' the 'image of the invisible God, the firstborn of all creation,' would have appeared anyway 'when the time had fully come,' not then to redeem, but to rule gloriously over the com-pleted creation. —N. T. Wright, *Paul and the Faithfulness of God*[45]

But even in Wright's own summary of what God did through Israel, I see a challenge to seeing any fall or any stumbling as a good thing. He explains:

> The Israelites were 'entrusted' with God's oracles, but *if* some proved unfaithful, that cannot nullify God's faithfulness, for God will be true even if every human is false. In other words, God will work through Israel for the salvation of the world, even though Israel as a whole will turn away. What's more, indeed, God will work through Israel's large-scale turning away for the salvation of the world! This, Paul is saying, is what has now been accomplished.[46]

"*If* some proved unfaithful." That's when he will use unfaithfulness for his purposes. Only *if* they do prove unfaithful. But this was not the original intention or plan of God—that is clear in the story as it develops—so we need to find other ways to explain what seem to be contradictions to this.

Our loving Father desired to see Israel thrive in the promised land, honoring him before the nations, and he deserved it. I cannot embrace a doctrine that celebrates the sad reality that he didn't get this.

I have to agree with Fleming Rutledge:

> Evil is in no way part of God's good purpose, and cannot be, since it does not have existence as a created good. Evil is neither rationally nor morally intelligible and must simply be loathed and resisted. The beginning of resistance is not to explain, but to see. Seeing is itself a form of action—seeing evil for what it is, not a part of God's plan, but a colossal x factor in creation, a monstrous contradiction, a prodigious negation that must be identified, denounced, and opposed wherever it occurs. —Fleming Rutledge, *The Crucifixion*[47]

Addendum 2

On Competing Narratives: A Reflection

This reflection was originally published on my church's website. This was the beginning of what later became Chapter 5 in this book.

I include this piece here to conclude the chapter, and the book, with a taste of the confusion and frustration I experienced for years about the state of affairs in the church in my generation. But it was this very state of affairs that motivated my efforts to find my way in God's world. This book is the first fruits of the first twelve years of work in that pursuit. If, in fact, the fruit is good, then this would be a great example of God using evil for good (see Addendum 1).

~

> *I speak as a member of a congregation whose founder was Abraham, and the name of my rabbi is Moses. I speak as a person who was able to leave Warsaw, the city in which I was born, just six weeks before the disaster began. My destination was New York, it would have been Auschwitz or Treblinka. I am a brand plucked from the fire, in which my people was burned to death.... I speak as a person who is often afraid and terribly alarmed lest God has turned away from [man] in disgust.* —Abraham Joshua Heschel[48]

Heschel, my friend, you are not alone. I often find myself afraid, and terribly alarmed. I think God *does* look in disgust, because even I often do, and I'm sure you did too. But about his giving up on us—the God of Hosea, Lamentations, and Isaiah—what are the chances?

*God does not stand outside the range of human
suffering and sorrow. He is personally involved in,
even stirred by, the conduct and fate of man.*
—Heschel, *The Prophets*[49]

*Comfort, comfort my people,
says your God.
Speak tenderly to Jerusalem...
You who bring good news to Zion,
go up on a high mountain.
You who bring good news to Jerusalem,
lift up your voice with a shout,
lift it up, do not be afraid;
say to the towns of Judah,
"Here is your God!"*
(Isaiah 40: 1–2, 9)

~

Undergirding the inexhaustible significance of the gospel is the reality, and the miracle, of *who God is*. I say "miracle" because it didn't have to be this way. Think about it. God could have been otherwise, an infinite range of alternatives to who he actually is. Reality could have been anything, from absolute nothingness, to all sorts of meaningless situations—or worse. But God is Love. We simply cannot imagine a better scenario as the background to our existence.

And yet, we love to entertain fantasies. We refuse to be at home in our own Story, to be onboard with our Creator. We want the forbidden fruit, to be like the nations, Baalism, syncretism, paganism, imperialism, nationalism, consumerism, careerism—a host of competing narratives and agendas, including the American Dream and all those alternative realities we so love to inhabit.

But we cannot resist the Spirit and the Word of God forever. That thick cloud of witnesses. That multitude of voices gushing to us from the past like the sound of rushing waters.

> *This is what is written: The Messiah will suffer and rise from the dead on the third day, and repentance for the forgiveness of sins will be preached in his name to all nations, beginning at Jerusalem.* (Luke 24:46–47)

Repentance for the forgiveness of sins. Doors wide open to return to our Creator and embrace the very reason we exist. An invitation that reminds us of the price he had to pay to set us free. But free for what? To indulge in all the nonsense that led us astray and got us condemned in the first place? To go about the land of the living as if God didn't have an agenda for his creation? No. As much creative freedom as the Lord has given us, his invitation is still from darkness to light, to share in his own life, which was his intention from the beginning.

> *To throw open the circulatory movement of the divine light and the divine relationships, and to take men and women, with the whole of creation, into the lifestream of the triune God: that is the meaning of creation, reconciliation and glorification.* —Jürgen Moltmann[50]

The fierce Love that fires the sun is making his home among us. And there's no place to hide from the light of truth, the need for humility, and the call for justice. Reality is holy ground.[51]

---

[1] Alister McGrath, *If I Had Lunch with C. S. Lewis: Exploring the Ideas of C. S. Lewis on the Meaning of Life* (Carol Stream, IL: Tyndale House Publishers, 2014), p. 70.

[2] I elaborate on this in ch. 1, under "A Biblical Metaphysic."

[3] John G. Stackhouse Jr., *Making the Best of It: Following Christ in the Real World* (New York: Oxford University Press, 2008), p. 352.

[4] Christopher J. H. Wright, *The Mission of God's People: A Biblical Theology of the Church's Mission* (Grand Rapids: Zondervan, 2010).

[5] Andy Crouch, *Culture Making: Recovering Our Creative Calling* (Downers Grove: IVP Books, 2008); Peter L. Berger and Thomas Luckmann, *The Social Construction of Reality: A Treatise in the Sociology of Knowledge* (New York: Anchor, 1967); Terence E. Fretheim, *God and World in the Old Testament: A Relational Theology of Creation* (Nashville: Abingdon Press, 2005). See also ch. 1, under "The Social Construction of Reality."

[6] George W. Stroup, *The Promise of Narrative Theology* (Eugene, OR: Wipf & Stock, 1997), p. 258: "The identity of Christian individuals and communities is finally rooted in and dependent on the yet unfinished narrative in which God has his identity in relation to the world. Christian hope, therefore, is based not on a repetition of the past, but on the expectation of a future in which God's promises in the past will be consummated in new and unexpected ways. Christians look to the future not simply as a repetition of the past, but as the final, yet undisclosed, meaning of the past and the present."

[7] This is a transcript I edited from a promotional video for David Platt's book *Radical: Taking Back Your Faith from the American Dream* (Colorado Springs: Multnomah, 2010). For the video, see "Radical by David Platt," directed by Taylor Robinson, accessed April 20, 2020, 2:07, https://vimeo.com/11348896. Some reviewers have complained that in this book Platt is overemphasizing some areas of "mission" over other ways in which we embody the gospel. But why am I not surprised! This is a tendency that seems quite common in the church more broadly: each denomination overemphasizing their own strengths, while refusing to learn from the strengths of others.

[8] See Andrew Delbanco, *The Real American Dream: A Meditation on Hope* (Cambridge, MA: Harvard University Press, 1999): "The history of hope I have tried to sketch in this book is one of diminution. At first, the self expanded toward (and was sometimes overwhelmed by) the vastness of

God. From the early republic to the Great Society, it remained implicated in a national ideal lesser than God but larger and more enduring than any individual citizen. Today, hope has narrowed to the vanishing point of the self alone" (p. 103).

[9] See ch. 2.

[10] The word of the LORD through Jeremiah—"For surely I know the plans I have for you, says the LORD, plans for your welfare and not for harm, to give you a future with hope" (Jer 29:11 NRSV)—though typically read in individualistic terms, is actually part of a letter to the nation of Israel when it was in exile in Babylon. It's not a word originally meant for individual readers of this text. Although these words do have implications for us—God remains the same and we *are* the people of God, and though the Spirit can and does use these very words to encourage any one of us at any given time, the point remains that the gospel is not *about me*—it's a cosmic reality that we're invited into. Does not God love us then, and have a wonderful plan for our lives? He sure does, but that plan includes picking up our cross if we want to be part of his family: "Whoever wants to be my disciple *must* deny themselves and take up their cross and follow me. For whoever wants to save their life will lose it, but whoever loses their life for me will find it" (Matt 16:24–25). That bit is part of the gospel too, but it's a *good* thing only because of the Story in which it makes sense—the biblical Story. Part of what we'll try to make sense of in this project is why God has chosen to tackle evil in such a sacrificial, cross-bearing, way. I'm sure he has good reasons if he's willing to pay such a price himself.

[11] For a fairly recent exposition of these tendencies (among other things), see Christine Jeske, "This Pandemic Hits Americans Where We're Spiritually Weak," Christianity Today, May 7, 2020, https://www.christianitytoday. com/ct/2020/may-web-only/coronavirus-pandemic-hits-americans-spiritually-weak.html.

[12] Dietrich Bonhoeffer, *Letters and Papers from Prison* (London: SCM Press, 2001), p. 33.

[13] See J. Richard Middleton, "Creation Founded in Love: Breaking Rhetorical Expectations in Genesis 1:1–2:3," in *Sacred Text, Secular Times: The Hebrew Bible in the Modern World*, eds. Leonard Jay Greenspoon and Bryan F LeBeau (Omaha NE: Creighton University Press, 2000).

[14] Notice that in the Old Testament God only asked that we love our neighbor *as ourselves* (Lev 19:18). If you think about it, that isn't much to ask. It's only that we treat others as we want to be treated ourselves. But this changes in the

New Testament. Now we have a "new commandment" to love one another *as he has loved us* (John 13:34; 15:12 NRSV). And how has he loved us? Well, he gave his life for us (cf. John 15:13)! Can you see what this means? At the beginning he made sure we knew we should take care of ourselves and love ourselves, but now it's as if he was saying: "you know, just forget about yourselves and be *for others,* just as I am for others—even my enemies" (see Matt 5:43–48; Rom 5:8,10). This for-otherness is a natural expression of the "image" and "likeness" of God (Gen 1:26–27; 1 John 4:7–9), and it's now our aim as disciples of the Son of God.

[15] This tendency is also played out in the political arena in the U.S. See Andy Stanley, *Not in It to Win It: Why Choosing Sides Sidelines the Church* (Grand Rapids: Zondervan Reflective, 2022).

[16] See the explanation by Ted Turnau below, under the sub-section "Popular Culture," in relationship to popular culture and its effects on us at the level of worldview.

[17] James K. A. Smith, *Desiring the Kingdom: Worship, Worldview, and Cultural Formation* (Grand Rapids: Baker Academic, 2009).

[18] N. T. Wright, *Creation, Power and Truth: The Gospel in a World of Cultural Confusion* (London: SPCK, 2013).

[19] Walter Brueggemann, *The Prophetic Imagination*, 2nd ed. (Minneapolis: Augsburg Fortress Publishers, 2001), p. 11.

[20] Juan M. Floyd-Thomas, Stacey M. Floyd-Thomas, and Mark G. Toulouse, *The Altars Where We Worship: The Religious Significance of Popular Culture* (Louisville, KY: Westminster John Knox Press, 2016), p. 1.

[21] Ibid., pp. 6–7. They explain that "Like more formal religions, each of these altars provides followers with (1) a mythic narrative to aid in addressing matters of sacred meaning and holy significance, sometimes in epic fashion; (2) a system of doctrines that outlines appropriate relationships and offers guidance concerning how followers should orient themselves within the world; (3) a set of ethical codes defining key values, principles or precepts, and rules or laws; (4) an organization or institution to aid in perpetuating religious ideas and imbedding them in the societal fabric; (5) a ritualistic dimension within which the faithful engage in acts that define meaning for life and merge belief with exercises of experience and practice; (6) an experiential dimension that enables followers to express their feelings and experience extraordinary meaning; and (7) a material dimension with concrete and tangible expressions of the sacred that enliven the five senses of touch, smell, sight, hearing, and taste."

[22] Ralph C. Wood, *Contending for the Faith: The Church's Engagement with Culture* (Waco, TX: Baylor University Press, 2003), pp. 1–2.

[23] J. Richard Middleton and Brian J. Walsh, *Truth Is Stranger Than It Used to Be: Biblical Faith in a Postmodern Age* (Downers Grove: IVP Academic, 1995), pp. 183–4.

[24] For more on this, see ch. 4: "Life in the Spirit"

[25] Ted Turnau, *Popologetics,* "Introduction," under section "Responding to the Worldview Challenge," Kindle ed.

[26] See Paul M. Gould, *Cultural Apologetics: Renewing the Christian Voice, Conscience, and Imagination in a Disenchanted World* (Grand Rapids: Zondervan Academic, 2019).

[27] Ted Turnau, *Popologetics,* "Introduction," under section "Responding to the Worldview Challenge," Kindle ed.

[28] See especially J. Richard Middleton, *A New Heaven and a New Earth: Reclaiming Biblical Eschatology* (Grand Rapids: Baker Academic, 2014), where he not only explains the biblical vision of cosmic renewal, but also finds solutions to "problem texts," texts that seem to suggest cosmic destruction and otherworldly hope instead. See also N. T. Wright, *Surprised by Hope: Rethinking Heaven, the Resurrection, and the Mission of the Church* (New York: HarperOne, 2008); and more recently, James Paul, *What on Earth Is Heaven?* (London: InterVarsity Press, 2021).

[29] Middleton, *A New Heaven and a New Earth*, p. 283ff. In the Appendix "Whatever Happened to the New Earth?" Middleton offers a helpful summary of the history of eschatology. And it seems that he's working on a book-length study on it (p. 283, n. 1).

[30] Ibid., pp. 311–12.

[31] The issues I see here are related to those I mentioned regarding Christian eschatology, in that they're both expressions of the broader issue of Christian dualism: our tendencies to devalue everyday life and the world of space, time and matter, typically in the hope of "heaven" or some higher realm. I limit my focus to these two issues because they're instances of dualism I personally wrestled with for years. For a helpful introduction to the problem and history of dualism, see Brian J. Walsh and J. Richard Middleton, *The Transforming Vision: Shaping a Christian World View* (Downers Grove: IVP Academic, 1984), chs. 6 and 7. See also Middleton, *A New Heaven and a New Earth,* ch. 1 ("Introduction: The Problem of Otherworldly Hope");

George Eldon Ladd, *The Pattern of New Testament Truth* (Grand Rapids: Wm. B. Eerdmans Publishing, 1968), ch. 1 ("The Background of the Pattern: Greek or Hebrew?"); and Os Guinness, *The Call: Finding and Fulfilling the Central Purpose of Your Life* (Nashville: W. Publishing Group, 1998), ch. 4 ("Everyone, Everywhere, Everything").

[32] José Soto, "Our Sense of Self," Wayfinders, December 25, 2020, https://www.wayfinders.quest/sense-of-self.html.

[33] See Leisa Aitken, "All in the Mind? Psychology, Mindfulness and Christianity," Centre for Public Christianity, March 25, 2013, https://www.publicchristianity.org/all-in-the-mind-psychology-mindfulness-and-christianity/.

[34] Daniel J. Siegel, *Mindsight: The New Science of Personal Transformation* (New York: Bantam, 2010), esp. ch. 4, "The Complexity Choir: Discovering the Harmony of Health."

[35] See especially Mark Williams and Danny Penman, *Mindfulness: An Eight-Week Plan for Finding Peace in a Frantic World* (New York: Rodale Books, 2011). For Prof. Mark Williams' bio, visit https://www.neuroscience.ox.ac.uk/research-directory/mark-williams.

[36] On my view of reality as one, see ch. 1, under section "The Lens of Our Experience."

[37] For a very helpful exploration of this topic in general, one very much in line with what I see and what I think needs attention, see Jürgen Moltmann, *The Living God and the Fullness of Life* (Louisville, KY: Westminster John Knox Press, 2015), ch. 9, "A Spirituality of the Senses."

[38] Here's my favorite version of the Examen: https://www.wayfinders.quest/examen.html.

[39] For example, I see much confusion around the question of godly masculinity. I recently read Kristin Kobes Du Mez's *Jesus and John Wayne: How White Evangelicals Corrupted a Faith and Fractured a Nation* (New York: Liveright Publishing, 2020), and I think it's an important contribution to our understanding of our times and evangelical Christianity in particular. At this point, my sense is that her account of evangelical masculinity is pretty much right-on: it paints an unfortunate and very disturbing picture, but it does help explain a lot that has puzzled me for years, especially the unkindness and the arrogant attitudes and behavior of so many men claiming to be followers of Christ—myself included. However, if this conversation is to be constructive and helpful to all involved, I think we would also benefit from a robust

and convincing account of *biblical* masculinity, one that could potentially replace the caricatures we have come to embrace. Now, I think it should be obvious that there's more than one kind or style of masculinity that would be pleasing to God, so it might be best to think in terms of the *parameters* of biblical masculinity when inquiring into this subject: What sorts of attitudes, postures, and ways of being a man are compatible with the nature and character of the One in whose image we're made?

[40] Under section "A Biblical Metaphysic."

[41] Here's the song at her website: https://www.audreyassad.com/fortunate-fall.

[42] My classmate's words. On Leibniz's account, see Brandon C. Look, ed., *The Bloomsbury Companion to Leibniz* (London: Bloomsbury Academic, 2014), p. 202ff.; and Larry M. Jorgensen and Samuel Newlands, eds., *New Essays on Leibniz's Theodicy* (New York: Oxford University Press, 2014).

[43] See my initial reflections and my sources on this: https://www.wayfinders.quest/spiritual-dimension.html.

[44] See, for example, J. Richard Middleton, "From Primal Harmony to a Broken World: Distinguishing God's Intent for Life from the Encroachment of Death in Genesis 2–3," in *Earnest: Interdisciplinary Work Inspired by the Life and Teachings of B. T. Roberts*, eds. Andrew C. Koehl and David Basinger (Eugene, OR: Pickwick, 2017), p. 159, n. 48: "We should note that there is a negation ('not') used in the prohibition against eating from this tree [of the knowledge of good and evil], which is reflected in the proliferation of negations in the conversation the snake and the woman have about the tree (Gen 3:1–5) and also in YHWH God's later mention of the tree (Gen 3:11, 17). When read with the two other sets of negations (about the *lack* of vegetation on the land; the *lack* of a companion for the human), we might think that this negation about eating from the tree likewise indicates a lack *that should be remedied*. And some interpreters have, indeed, read the story as a Fall 'upwards' or 'forwards,' into maturity, as if the humans *needed* to eat from this tree in order to attain their full potential as adults. This is a tempting reading, but it is contradicted by the tragic outcome of the eating, where human life becomes diminished and constricted; this diminishing of life confirms that the prohibition should have been respected." See also Terence E. Fretheim, *The Suffering of God: An Old Testament Perspective* (Minneapolis: Fortress Press, 1984).

[45] N. T. Wright, *Paul and the Faithfulness of God* (Minneapolis: Fortress Press, 2013), p. 1210.

[46] Ibid., p. 1208 (emphasis mine).

[47] Fleming Rutledge, *The Crucifixion: Understanding the Death of Jesus Christ* (Grand Rapids: Wm. B. Eerdmans Publishing, 2015), p. 434.

[48] Abraham Joshua Heschel, *I Asked for Wonder: A Spiritual Anthology*, ed. Samuel H. Dresner (New York: The Crossroad Publishing Company, 1983), p. 93.

[49] Heschel, *The Prophets* (New York: Harper & Row, 1962), p. 289.

[50] Jürgen Moltmann, *The Trinity and the Kingdom* (Minneapolis: Fortress Press, 1993), p. 178.

[51] I borrowed the phrase "[the] fierce Love who fires the sun" from Steven Bouma-Prediger and Brian J. Walsh, *Beyond Homelessness: Christian Faith in a Culture of Displacement* (Grand Rapids: Wm. B. Eerdmans Publishing, 2008), p. 304.

Afterword

Reality is holy ground. I think we can say that with confidence after all we have learned about reality according to the Scriptures.

But what does "holy" mean? What was it that Moses saw when the Holy One of Israel revealed himself on the mountain (Exod 33:18–19)? He saw his "goodness." To say that God is holy, at bottom, is to say that God is good (34:5–7): compassionate, gracious, slow to anger, abounding in steadfast love and faithfulness, just—in short, he is good.[1]

He also created *us* good—indeed, "very good" (Gen 1). We made a mess of things, yes, and filled the earth with filth. But the rest of the Story shows us how committed God is to his vision for the work of his hands. To his vision for *us*. He made us to be his intimate allies in the making of this world. And he hasn't given up on it. Believe it or not, it is happening. Reality is indeed holy ground.

The reality is that this is God's world; and we are his children. And "children," in God's *new world* (in his "kingdom"), means to be one with him, to be *his* agents, enacting his vision for the world.

Let us not forget that he's already *in* us (1 Cor 6:19–20). Which means that he *lives* in us. Which means that he wants to live *through* us.

---

[1] Goodness obviously doesn't exhaust the meaning of holiness, but it is at the heart of it. Old Testament scholar Iain Provan would even say that "holiness is simply goodness by another name." Iain Provan, *Seeking What Is Right: The Old Testament and the Good Life* (Waco, TX: Baylor University Press, 2020), p. 5. See also this excellent series of blogs by Craig B. Larson, "Holy Means Good," *Knowing God and His Ways* (blog), August 13, 2018, https://craigbrianlarson.com/holy-means-good/.

Let us not forget that when we face the world, it is him facing the world, not just us. That when we face each other, it is him we're seeing, not just each other. That when the world sees us, it is him they're seeing—or at least, they should.

But do we really want this? Do we trust him enough, and love him enough, to actually want to be one with him? Let us pray about that. Let us look into that, and work on that.

Friends, thanks for reflecting with me about all I brought up in these pages. As I said in the Introduction, the rest of this project will seek to sort out the questions raised in this volume, and much more.

The next volume in the series is projected to be a collaborative study, a collection of short essays and reflections written by a transdenominational team of contributors. The aim of that book is to test, clarify, and develop the vision proposed in the present volume.

The rest of the series will continue to test, build, and expand on what we have learned so far, until we're ready for the last volume, which is projected to be a full-fledged discipleship manual, including resources to support our witness to the goodness of God and of his ways.

Reality is God's Story, and he's given us a crucial role to play. We owe it to the next generation of Christians to play our part well.

Come on church, let's set them up for success—the Lord deserves it. Let's get our eyes off ourselves, that we may share the culture of heaven on earth.

What would *that* look like? Let's do it and see.

BIBLIOGRAPHY

Alexander, Philip. "'The Agent of the King Is Treated as the King Himself': Does the Worship of Jesus Imply His Divinity?" In *In the Fullness of Time: Essays on Christology, Creation, and Eschatology in Honor of Richad Bauckham,* edited by Daniel M. Gurtner, Grant Macaskill, and Jonathan T. Pennington. Grand Rapids: Wm. "B. Eerdmans Publishing, 2016."

Alexander, T. Desmond. "Promises, Divine." In *Dictionary of the Old Testament: Pentateuch,* edited by T. Desmond Alexander and David W. Baker. Downers Grove: IVP Academic, 2002.

Alston, William P. *Perceiving God: The Epistemology of Religious Experience.* Ithaca, NY: Cornell University Press, 1993.

Archer, Margaret S., Andrew Collier, and Douglas V. Porpora. "What Do We Mean by God?" In *Transcendence: Critical Realism and God.* New York: Routledge, 2004.

Bauckham, Richard. *Gospel of Glory: Major Themes in Johannine Theology.* Grand Rapids: Baker Academic, 2015.

Beale, G. K. *A New Testament Biblical Theology: The Unfolding of the Old Testament in the New.* Baker Academic, 2011.

Beale, G. K., and Mitchell Kim. *God Dwells Among Us: Expanding Eden to the Ends of the Earth.* IVP Books, 2014.

Berger, Peter L., and Thomas Luckmann. *The Social Construction of Reality: A Treatise in the Sociology of Knowledge.* New York: Anchor, 1967.

Blocher, Henri. "Agnus Victor: The Atonement as Victory and Vicarious Punishment." In *What Does It Mean to Be Saved? Broadening Evangelical Horizons of Salvation,* edited by John G. Stackhouse Jr. Grand Rapids: Baker Academic, 2002.

————. *In the Beginning: The Opening Chapters of Genesis.* Downers Grove: IVP, 1984.

Bock, Darrell L. *A Theology of Luke and Acts: God's Promised Program, Realized for All Nations.* Grand Rapids: Zondervan, 2012.

————. *Recovering the Real Lost Gospel: Reclaiming the Gospel as Good News.* Nashville: B&H Academic, 2010.

Boersma, Hans, and Rikk E. Watts. *Athens and Jerusalem: Philosophy and History Informing Christian Theol.* Regent College, Vancouver [BC, Canada], 2009. https://www.regentaudio.com/products/athens-and-jerusalem-philosophy-and-history-informing-christian-theology-a-dialogue.

Bonhoeffer, Dietrich. *Letters and Papers from Prison.* London: SCM Press, 2001.

Bouma-Prediger, Steven, and Brian J. Walsh. *Beyond Homelessness: Christian Faith in a Culture of Displacement.* Grand Rapids: Wm. B. Eerdmans Publishing, 2008.

Brown, William P. *Sacred Sense: Discovering the Wonder of God's Word and World.* Grand Rapids: Wm. B. Eerdmans Publishing, 2015.

————. *The Ethos of the Cosmos: The Genesis of Moral Imagination in the Bible.* Grand Rapids: Wm. B. Eerdmans Publishing Co., 1999.

————. *The Seven Pillars of Creation: The Bible, Science, and the Ecology of Wonder.* New York: Oxford University Press, 2010.

Bruce, F. F. *The Gospel of John: Introduction, Exposition, Notes.* 3rd ed. Grand Rapids: Wm. B. Eerdmans Publishing, 1994.

Brueggemann, Walter. *The Prophetic Imagination.* Second Edition. Minneapolis, MN: Augsburg Fortress Publishers, 2001.

Clifford, Richard J., ed. *Wisdom Literature in Mesopotamia and Israel*. Society of Biblical Literature Symposium Series 36. Atlanta: Society of Biblical Literature, 2007.

Colijn, Brenda B. *Images of Salvation in the New Testament*. Downers Grove: IVP Academic, 2010.

Crouch, Andy. *Culture Making: Recovering Our Creative Calling*. Downers Grove: IVP, 2013.

Dahlberg, Karin, Helena Dahlberg, and Maria Nystrom. *Reflective Lifeworld Research*. 2nd ed. Lund: Studentlitteratur AB, 2008.

Delbanco, Andrew. *The Real American Dream: A Meditation on Hope*. Cambridge, MA: Harvard University Press, 1999.

deSilva, David A. *The Letter to the Galatians*. Grand Rapids: Wm. B. Eerdmans Publishing, 2018.

———. *Transformation: The Heart of Paul's Gospel*. Bellingham, WA: Lexham Press, 2014.

Dickson, John. *A Doubter's Guide to the Bible: Inside History's Bestseller for Believers and Skeptics*. Grand Rapids: Zondervan, 2014.

Du Mez, Kristin Kobes. *Jesus and John Wayne: How White Evangelicals Corrupted a Faith and Fractured a Nation*. New York: Liveright Publishing, 2020.

Eagleton, Terry. *The Meaning of Life: A Very Short Introduction*. New York: Oxford University Press, 2008.

Evans, Mary J. "Blessing/Curse." In *New Dictionary of Biblical Theology: Exploring the Unity Diversity of Scripture*, edited by Brian S. Rosner, T. Desmond Alexander, Graeme Goldsworthy, and D. A. Carson. Downers Grove: IVP Academic, 2000.

Fee, Gordon D. *God's Empowering Presence: The Holy Spirit in the Letters of Paul*. Grand Rapids: Baker Academic, 2009.

———. *Paul, the Spirit, and the People of God*. Grand Rapids: Baker Academic, 1996.

Fitzmyer, Joseph A. *The Gospel According to Luke I–IX: Introduction, Translation, and Notes*. Garden City, NY: Doubleday, 1981.

Floyd-Thomas, Juan M., Stacey M. Floyd-Thomas, and Mark G. Toulouse. *The Altars Where We Worship: The Religious Significance of Popular Culture*. Louisville: Westminster John Knox Press, 2016.

Ford, David F. *The Drama of Living: Becoming Wise in the Spirit*. Grand Rapids: Brazos Press, 2014.

Frankl, Viktor E. *Man's Search for Meaning*. 4th ed. Boston, MA: Beacon Press, 2000.

———. *Man's Search for Ultimate Meaning*. Rev. ed. Cambridge, MA: Basic Books, 2000.

———. *The Feeling of Meaninglessness. A Challenge to Psychotherapy and Philosophy*. Edited by Alexander Batthyany. Milwaukee, WI: Marquette University Press, 2010.

Fretheim, Terence E. *God and World in the Old Testament: A Relational Theology of Creation*. Nashville: Abingdon Press, 2005.

———. *The Suffering of God: An Old Testament Perspective*. Minneapolis: Fortress Press, 1984.

Gabriel, Andrew K. "The Holy Spirit and Eschatology—with Implications for Ministry and the Doctrine of Spirit Baptism." *Journal of Pentecostal Theology* 25, no. 2 (Sept. 10, 2016): 203–21. https://doi.org/10.1163/17455251-02502004.

Garber, Steven. *The Fabric of Faithfulness: Weaving Together Belief and Behavior*. Downers Grove: IVP, 2007.

Gentry, Peter J., and Stephen J. Wellum. *Kingdom through Covenant: A Biblical-Theological Understanding of the Covenants*. Wheaton: Crossway, 2012.

Goldingay, John. *Do We Need the New Testament?: Letting the Old Testament Speak for Itself*. Downers Grove: IVP Academic, 2015.

Goldsworthy, Graeme, Dane C. Ortlund, and Miles V. Van Pelt. *The Son of God and the New Creation.* Short Studies in Biblical Theology. Wheaton: Crossway, 2015.

Gould, Paul M. *Cultural Apologetics: Renewing the Christian Voice, Conscience, and Imagination in a Disenchanted World.* Grand Rapids: Zondervan Academic, 2019.

Greenspoon, Leonard Jay, and Bryan F. LeBeau, eds. *Sacred Text, Secular Times: The Hebrew Bible in the Modern World.* Omaha, NE: Creighton University Press, 2000.

Gregersen, Niels Henrik, Bengt Kristensson Uggla, and Trygve Wyller, eds. *Reformation Theology for a Post-Secular Age: Logstrup, Prenter, Wingren, and the Future of Scandinavian Creation Theology.* Göttingen: Vandenhoeck & Ruprecht, 2017.

Guinness, Os. *The Call: Finding and Fulfilling the Central Purpose of Your Life.* Nashville: W. Publishing Group, 1998.

Hall, Christopher. *The Role of Tradition in Evangelical Theology.* Regent College, Vancouver [BC, Canada], 2005. https://www.regentaudio.com/products/the-role-of-tradition-in-evangelical-theology.

Harink, Douglas. *Apocalyptic and the Future of Theology: With and Beyond J. Louis Martyn.* Edited by Joshua B. Davis. Eugene, OR: Cascade Books, 2012.

Hays, Richard. *The Moral Vision of the New Testament: Community, Cross, New Creation: A Contemporary Introduction to New Testament Ethic.* San Francisco: HarperOne, 1996.

———. *Echoes of Scripture in the Letters of Paul.* New Haven: Yale University Press, 1993.

Heiser, Michael S. *Supernatural: What the Bible Teaches About the Unseen World—and Why It Matters.* Bellingham: Lexham Press, 2015.

———. *Demons: What the Bible Really Says About the Powers of Darkness.* Bellingham, WA: Lexham Press, 2020.

————. *The Unseen Realm: Recovering the Supernatural Worldview of the Bible.* Bellingham: Lexham Press, 2015.

Held, Shai. *Abraham Joshua Heschel: The Call of Transcendence.* Bloomington, IN: Indiana University Press, 2015.

Heschel, Abraham J. *Man Is Not Alone: A Philosophy of Religion.* New York: Farrar, Straus and Giroux, 1979.

————. *The Prophets.* New York: Harper & Row, 1962.

Holland, Tom. *Dominion: How the Christian Revolution Remade the World.* New York: Basic Books, 2019.

Holmes, Christopher R. J. "The Spirit and the Promise: On Becoming Aligned with the Way Things Really Are." In *Apocalyptic and the Future of Theology: With and Beyond J. Louis Martyn,* edited by Joshua B. Davis and Douglas Harink, 219–35. Eugene, OR: Cascade Books, 2012.

Horton, Michael. *The Christian Faith: A Systematic Theology for Pilgrims on the Way.* Grand Rapids: Zondervan, 2011.

Husbands, Mark, ed. *Ancient Faith for the Church's Future.* Downers Grove: IVP Academic, 2008.

Jennings, Timothy R. *The God-Shaped Brain: How Changing Your View of God Transforms Your Life.* Downers Grove: IVP, 2017.

Johnson, Adam J. *The Reconciling Wisdom of God: Reframing the Doctrine of the Atonement.* Bellingham: Lexham Press, 2016.

Jorgensen, Larry M., and Samuel Newlands, eds. *New Essays on Leibniz's Theodicy.* New York: Oxford University Press, 2014.

Judge, Edwin. "How the Debate Between Rome & Jerusalem Shaped the Modern World." Accessed February 17, 2022. https://www.gospelconversations.com/series/edwin-judge.

Keener, Craig S. *The Gospel of John: Two Volumes*. Grand Rapids: Baker Academic, 2010.

Kelsey, David H. *Eccentric Existence: A Theological Anthropology*. Louisville, KY: Westminster John Knox Press, 2009.

Kettle, David J. *Western Culture in Gospel Context: Towards the Conversion of the West: Theological Bearings for Mission and Spirituality*. Cascade Books, 2014.

Kidner, F. Derek. "Isaiah." In *New Bible Commentary*, edited by Gordon J. Wenham, J. Alec Motyer, D. A. Carson, and R. T. France, 21st Century ed. Downers Grove: IVP Academic, 1994.

Koester, Craig R. *The Word of Life: A Theology of John's Gospel*. Grand Rapids: Wm. B. Eerdmans Publishing, 2008.

Ladd, George Eldon. *The Pattern of New Testament Truth*. Grand Rapids: Wm. B. Eerdmans Publishing, 1968.

Larson, Craig B. "Holy Means Good." *Knowing God and His Ways* (blog), August 13, 2018. https://craigbrianlarson.com/holy-means-good/.

Levison, Jack. *Boundless God*. Grand Rapids: Baker Academic, 2020.

———. *Filled with the Spirit*. Grand Rapids: Wm. B. Eerdmans Publishing, 2009.

———. *Inspired: The Holy Spirit and the Mind of Faith*. Grand Rapids: Wm. B. Eerdmans Publishing, 2013.

Lindbeck, George A. *The Nature of Doctrine, 25th Anniversary Edition: Religion and Theology in a Postliberal Age*. Louisville: Westminster John Knox Press, 2009.

Logstrup, Knud Eiler. *The Ethical Demand*. Edited by Hans Fink and Alasdair MacIntyre. Repr. ed. Notre Dame: University of Notre Dame Press, 1997.

Lonergan, Bernard. *Method in Theology: Lonergan Studies*. 2nd ed. Toronto, ON: University of Toronto Press, 2017.

Look, Brandon C., ed. *The Bloomsbury Companion to Leibniz.* London: Bloomsbury Academic, 2014.

Manen, Max van. *Phenomenology of Practice: Meaning-Giving Methods in Phenomenological Research and Writing.* New York: Routledge, 2014.

————, ed. *Writing in the Dark: Phenomenological Studies in Interpretive Inquiry.* New York: Routledge, 2003.

McConville, J. Gordon. *Being Human in God's World: An Old Testament Theology of Humanity.* Grand Rapids: Baker Academic, 2016.

McGrath, Alister. *If I Had Lunch with C. S. Lewis: Exploring the Ideas of C. S. Lewis on the Meaning of Life.* Carol Stream, IL: Tyndale House Publishers, 2014.

————. *Re-Imagining Nature: The Promise of a Christian Natural Theology.* Chichester, West Sussex: John Wiley & Sons, 2017.

Meek, Esther Lightcap. *Contact with Reality: Michael Polanyi's Realism and Why It Matters.* Eugene, OR: Cascade Books, 2017.

Merleau-Ponty, Maurice. *Phenomenology of Perception.* Translated by Donald Landes. New York: Routledge, 2012.

Middleton, J. Richard. *A New Heaven and a New Earth: Reclaiming Biblical Eschatology.* Grand Rapids: Baker Academic, 2014.

————. "A Sacred Calling for Sacred Work." Making All Things New conference, Center for Faith & Work, Redeemer Presbyterian Church, New York City. November 8, 2014. https://vimeo.com/118729385.

————. "Creation Founded in Love: Breaking Rhetorical Expectations in Genesis 1:1–2:3." In *Sacred Text, Secular Times: The Hebrew Bible in the Modern World*, edited by Leonard Jay Greenspoon and Bryan F LeBeau. Omaha, NE: Creighton University Press, 2000.

————. "From Primal Harmony to a Broken World: Distinguishing God's Intent for Life from the Encroachment of Death in Genesis 2–3." In *Earnest: Interdisciplinary Work Inspired by the Life and Teachings of B. T. Roberts*, edited by Andrew C. Koehl and David Basinger. Eugene, OR: Pickwick, 2017.

————. "The Blessing of Abraham and the Missio Dei: Reframing the Purpose of Israel's Election in Genesis 12:1-3." In *Orthodoxy and Orthopraxy: Essays in Tribute to Paul Livermore*, edited by Douglas R. Cullum and J. Richard Middleton. Eugene, OR: Pickwick Publications, 2020.

————. *The Liberating Image: The Imago Dei in Genesis 1*. Grand Rapids: Brazos Press, 2005.

Middleton, J. Richard, and Brian J. Walsh. *Truth Is Stranger Than It Used to Be: Biblical Faith in a Postmodern Age*. Downers Grove: IVP Academic, 1995.

Moltmann, Jürgen. *The Living God and the Fullness of Life*. Louisville, KY: Westminster John Knox Press, 2015.

————. *The Trinity and the Kingdom*. Minneapolis: Fortress Press, 1993.

Newman, Barclay Moon, and Philip C. Stine. *A Handbook on the Gospel of Matthew*. UBS Helps for Translators. New York: United Bible Societies, 1992.

Olson, Roger E. *The Essentials of Christian Thought: Seeing Reality through the Biblical Story*. Grand Rapids: Zondervan, 2017.

Olthuis, James. *The Beautiful Risk*. Grand Rapids: Zondervan, 2001.

Ortlund, Gavin. "Image of Adam, Son of God: Genesis 5:3 and Luke 3:38 in Intercanonical Dialogue." *Journal of the Evangelical Theological Society* 57, no. 4 (December 2014): 673–88.

Parks, Sharon Daloz. *Big Questions, Worthy Dreams: Mentoring Emerging Adults in Their Search for Meaning, Purpose, and Faith.* Rev. ed. San Francisco: Jossey-Bass, 2011.

Pannenberg, Wolfhart. *Systematic Theology.* Translated by Geoffrey W. Bromiley. Grand Rapids: Wm. B. Eerdmans Publishing, 1997.

Paul, James. *What on Earth Is Heaven?* London: InterVarsity Press, 2021.

Pennington, Jonathan T. *Jesus the Great Philosopher: Rediscovering the Wisdom Needed for the Good Life.* Grand Rapids: Brazos Press, 2020.

Phillips, J. B. *The New Testament in Modern English.* New York: Collins, 1972.

Plato. *The Republic.* Translated by Desmond Lee. London: Penguin Classics, 2007.

Platt, David. *Radical: Taking Back Your Faith from the American Dream.* Colorado Springs: Multnomah, 2010.

Polanyi, Michael. *The Tacit Dimension.* Gloucester, MA: Peter Smith, 1983.

Provan, Iain. *Seeking What Is Right: The Old Testament and the Good Life.* Waco, TX: Baylor University Press, 2020.

————. *Seriously Dangerous Religion: What the Old Testament Really Says and Why It Matters.* Waco, TX: Baylor University Press, 2014.

————. *The Reformation and the Right Reading of Scripture.* Waco, TX: Baylor University Press, 2017.

Ricoeur, Paul. *Time and Narrative.* 3 vols. Chicago: University of Chicago Press, 1984.

Rosner, Brian S. *Known by God: A Biblical Theology of Personal Identity.* Grand Rapids: Zondervan, 2017.

————. "Son of God at the Centre: Anthropology in Biblical-Theological Perspective." In *Anthropology and New Testament Theology*, edited by Jason Maston and Benjamin E. Reynolds. London: T&T Clark, 2018.

Rousseau, David, and Julie Billingham. "A Systematic Framework for Exploring Worldviews and Its Generalization as a Multi-Purpose Inquiry Framework." *Systems* 6, no. 3 (September 2018): 27. https://doi.org/10.3390/systems6030027.

Rutledge, Fleming. *The Crucifixion: Understanding the Death of Jesus Christ.* Grand Rapids: Wm. B. Eerdmans Publishing, 2015.

Scobie, Charles H. H. *The Ways of Our God: An Approach to Biblical Theology.* Grand Rapids: Wm. B. Eerdmans Publishing, 2002.

Seerveld, Calvin. *Rainbows for the Fallen World: Aesthetic Life and Artistic Task.* Downsview, ON: Toronto Tuppence Press, 1980.

Siegel, Daniel J. *Mindsight: The New Science of Personal Transformation.* New York: Bantam, 2010.

Smith, James K. A. *Awaiting the King: Reforming Public Theology* (Cultural Liturgies). Grand Rapids: Baker Academic, 2017.

———. *Desiring the Kingdom: Worship, Worldview, and Cultural Formation* (Cultural Liturgies). Grand Rapids: Baker Academic, 2009.

———. *Imagining the Kingdom: How Worship Works* (Cultural Liturgies). Grand Rapids: Baker Academic, 2013.

———. *You Are What You Love: The Spiritual Power of Habit.* Grand Rapids: Brazos, 2016.

Soto, José. "Intro to Wayfinders." Wayfinders, December 25, 2020. https://www.wayfinders.quest.

———. "Co-Writing God's Story." https://www.wayfinders.quest/co-writing-gods-story.html.

———. "Inhabiting God's Story: Initial Reflections." https://www.wayfinders.quest/gods-story-reflections.html.

———. "Life in the Spirit." https://www.wayfinders.quest/holy-spirit.html.

————. "On Ruach Elohim."
https://www.wayfinders.quest/on-ruach-elohim.html.
————. "On the Satan."
https://www.wayfinders.quest/on-the-satan.html.
————. "Our Sense of Self."
https://www.wayfinders.quest/sense-of-self.html.
————. "The Gospel."
https://www.wayfinders.quest/the-gospel.html.
————. "The Spiritual Dimension of Reality."
https://www.wayfinders.quest/spiritual-dimension.html.
————. "Inhabiting Reality."
https://www.wayfinders.quest/inhabiting-reality.html
————. "What Matters Most."
https://www.wayfinders.quest/what-matters-most.html.

Stackhouse, John G. Jr. *Making the Best of It: Following Christ in the Real Wrold.* New York: Oxford University Press, 2008.

Stanley, Andy. *Not in It to Win It: Why Choosing Sides Sidelines the Church.* Grand Rapids: Zondervan Reflective, 2022.

Stein, Robert H. *The Synoptic Problem: An Introduction.* Grand Rapids: Baker, 1987.

Strauss, Gideon. "Wonder, Heartbreak and Hope." Capital Commentary. Center for Public Justice, January 28, 2011. https://cpjustice.org/public/capital_commentary/article/836.

Stroup, George W. *The Promise of Narrative Theology.* Eugene, OR: Wipf & Stock, 1997.

Swinburne, Richard. *The Existence of God.* 2nd ed. New York: Clarendon Press, 2004.

Thompson, Marianne Meye. *The Promise of the Father: Jesus and God in the New Testament.* Louisville: Westminster John Knox Press, 2000.

Tolkien, J. R. R. *The Two Towers: Being the Second Part of the Lord of the Rings.* 2nd ed. Boston, MA: Houghton Mifflin Company, 1982.

Tomlin, Graham. *The Prodigal Spirit: The Trinity, the Church and the Future of the World*. London: Alpha International, 2012.

Tsumura, David T. "The Doctrine of Creation 'Ex Nihilo' and the Translation of 'Tōhû Wābōhû.'" In *Pentateuchal Traditions in the Late Second Temple Period: Proceedings of the International Workshop in Tokyo, August 28–31, 2007*, edited by Akio Moriya and Gohei Hata, 3–21. Boston: Brill, 2012.

Turnau, Ted. *Popologetics: Popular Culture in Christian Perspective*. Phillipsburg, NJ: P&R, 2012.

Van Leeuwen, Raymond C. "Cosmos, Temple, House: Building and Wisdom in Ancient Mesopotamia and Israel." In *From the Foundations to the Crenellations: Essays on Temple Building in the Ancient Near East and Hebrew Bible*, edited by Mark J. Boda and Jamie Novotny, 399–421. Alter Orient Und Altes Testament 366. Münster: Ugarit-Verlag, 2010.

VanGemeren, Willem A., and Andrew Abernethy. "The Spirit and the Future: A Canonical Approach." In *Presence, Power and Promise: The Role of the Spirit of God in the Old Testament*, edited by David G. Firth and Paul D. Wegner, 321–45. Downers Grove: IVP Academic, 2011.

Walsh, Brian J., and J. Richard Middleton. *The Transforming Vision: Shaping a Christian World View*. Downers Grove: IVP Academic, 1984.

Watts, Rikk E. *Jerusalem Versus Athens Revisited: Why the 21st Century Is the Most Christian*. Regent College, Vancouver [BC, Canada], 2015. https://www. regentaudio.com/products/jerusalem-versus-athens-revisited-why-the-21st-century-is-the-most-christian-and-the-most-confused.

———. "The New Exodus/New Creational Restoration of the Image of God." In *What Does It Mean to Be Saved?*

Broadening Evangelical Horizons of Salvation, edited by John G. Stackhouse Jr, 15–41. Grand Rapids: Baker Academic, 2002.

Wildman, Wesley J. "Ground-of-Being Theologies." In *The Oxford Handbook of Religion and Science,* edited by Philip Clayton, pp. 612–32. New York: Oxford University Press, 2006.

Williams, D. H. *Evangelicals and Tradition (Evangelical Ressourcement): The Formative Influence of the Early Church*. Grand Rapids: Baker Academic, 2005.

Williams, Mark, and Danny Penman. *Mindfulness: An Eight-Week Plan for Finding Peace in a Frantic World*. New York: Rodale Books, 2011.

Wingren, Gustaf. *Creation and Law*. Repr. ed. Eugene, OR: Wipf and Stock, 2003.

Witherington, Ben, III. *Biblical Theology: The Convergence of the Canon*. New York: Cambridge University Press, 2019.

Wood, David, ed. *On Paul Ricoeur: Narrative and Interpretation*. London: Routledge, 1991.

Wood, Ralph C. *Contending for the Faith: The Church's Engagement with Culture*. Waco, TX: Baylor University Press, 2003.

Wright, Andrew. *Christianity and Critical Realism: Ambiguity, Truth and Theological Literacy*. New York: Routledge, 2012.

————. *Religious Education and Critical Realism: Knowledge, Reality and Religious Literacy*. New York: Routledge, 2015.

Wright, Christopher J. H. *Knowing the Holy Spirit Through the Old Testament*. Downers Grove: IVP Academic, 2006.

————. *The Mission of God: Unlocking the Bible's Grand Narrative*. Downers Grove: IVP Academic, 2006.

————. *The Mission of God's People: A Biblical Theology of the Church's Mission*. Grand Rapids: Zondervan, 2010.

Wright, N. T. *Creation, Power and Truth: The Gospel in a World of Cultural Confusion*. London: SPCK Publishing, 2013.

———. *History and Eschatology: Jesus and the Promise of Natural Theology*. Waco, TX: Baylor University Press, 2019.

———. *Jesus and the Victory of God*. Christian Origins and the Question of God, Vol. 2. Minneapolis: Fortress Press, 1996.

———. *Luke for Everyone*. 2nd ed. Louisville, KY: Westminster John Knox Press, 2004.

———. *Paul and the Faithfulness of God*. Christian Origins and the Question of God, Vol. 4. Minneapolis: Fortress Press, 2013.

———. *Simply Christian: Why Christianity Makes Sense*. New York: HarperOne, 2010.

———. *Surprised by Hope: Rethinking Heaven, the Resurrection, and the Mission of the Church*. New York: HarperOne, 2008.

———. *The Day the Revolution Began: Reconsidering the Meaning of Jesus's Crucifixion*. San Francisco: HarperOne, 2016.

———. *The New Testament and the People God*. Christian Origins and The Question of God, Vol. 1. Minneapolis: Fortress Press, 1992.

Wright, N. T., and Michael F. Bird. *The New Testament in Its World: An Introduction to the History, Literature, and Theology of the First Christians*. Grand Rapids: Zondervan Academic, 2019.

Author Index

SUBJECT INDEX

God

God the Father, 13–14, 25, 29, 33, 47, 61, 63–66, 67–69, 78, 101, 103

God the Son, ix, x, 35, 36, 38, ch. 3, 53, 60–61, 63–65, 66, 69, 73, 76, 77, 80, 86, 88–89, 99, 101, 109, 111, 112

God the Spirit, 16–17, ch.4, 93–94, 106

Yahweh (and LORD), 46, 61, 65

God's Presence, ix, 36, ch. 4, 98

who God is, 17, 25, 29, 33, 105

knowledge of God, 46, 64, 80, 85, 94, 98, 115

intimacy with God, 25, 29, 63, 115

oneness with God, 61, 63, 64–70, 77

God's Story

God's Story, ix, 9, 10, 11, 13, 21, 22, 34–35, 36–37, ch. 3, 51, 56–59, 60, 116

God's world, 10, 11, 30, 85, 104, 115

God's vision, 66, 85, 89, 96

God's will, 36, 69, 85, 100

God's kingdom, 35–36, 38, 60, 80, 115

God's gospel, ix, x, 16, 17, ch. 2, 42, 51, 60, 67, 70, 72, 76, 83, 85, 87, 88–89, 99, 105, 107, 108

God's mission, 46, 52, 72, 79, 107

God's Word, 9, 40, 106

Scripture(s), x, 4, 21, 21, 31, 32, 34, 56, 59, 67, 73, 88, 89, 93, 115

Bible, the, ix, 3, 9, 13, 15, 21, 32, 40, 44, 51, 65, 67, 93

Old Testament, 15, 53, 54, 61, 73, 74, 107, 108

New Testament, 15, 16, 35, 36, 60, 73, 79, 102, 109

Gospels, 15, 25, 36, 38, 44

canon, 16, 41, 93

God's People

God's people, ix, x, 52, 53, 54, 57, 58, 61, 66, 72, 76, 85, 87, 95, 104–105, 108

children of God, 11, 30, 39, 44–45, 52, 68, 79, 87, 93, 115

new humanity, 45, 46, 57, 69, 70

SCRIPTURE INDEX